CONTENTS

About the Author .... *ii*

Foreword .... *vi*

Chapter 1 .... *1*

Chapter 2 .... *12*

Chapter 3 .... *24*

Chapter 4 .... *40*

Chapter 5 .... *50*

Chapter 6 .... *57*

Chapter 7 .... *67*

Chapter 8 .... *75*

Chapter 9 .... *93*

Chapter 10 .... *113*

Chapter 11 .... *128*

Chapter 12 .... *135*

Chapter 13 .... *151*

Acknowledgments *155*

Questions to Consider *157*

ABOUT THE AUTHOR

Ryan Wilkins is a devoted husband, a proud uncle, a protective brother, a skilled attorney, a fantasy-sports aficionado, and a good friend. His educational and leadership exploits range from the dignified (graduating from college with a perfect GPA; serving as Student Body President) to the slightly-less-so (ring-leading fraternity antics gone hilariously wrong; using the phrase "nuttier than squirrel poop" in a published article). Today, Ryan serves his church and community as a Stephen Minister and via his role on the Board of Directors for Ted E. Bear Hollow, a not-for-profit organization providing grief-support services to children who have lost loved ones.

On a more personal level, I have had the privilege of knowing Ryan since our freshman year of college. Over the years, I've witnessed his character in moments both big and small, in success and failure, in joy and in despair. Through it all, I've seen a man with a unique talent for pondering life's big questions in unexpected ways. Perhaps this ability is a reflection of Ryan's multifaceted personality, comprised of traits that might at first glance seem contradictory.

For instance, anyone who knows Ryan knows that he is intensely competitive. (I once witnessed Ryan wrestle a rival baseball team's homerun ball from the clutches of another bleacher-seat fan and chuck it back onto the field, only to embarrassingly realize his foe was just a dad trying to keep the ball for his son.) But alongside his competitive nature, Ryan is also known for his kind and compassionate spirit. I think of the time when, during a tough winter and amidst his own trials, Ryan opened his door to a homeless man in need of a warm bed. Likewise, Ryan is undoubtedly one of the smartest people I've ever met. This is a man who, on demand, can take any word given to him and immediately repeat it, backwards. For example, *grapefruit* becomes *tiurfeparg*, instantly. Yet despite possessing the talent, confidence, and wit to easily brand himself the center of attention, Ryan has a wonderful way of making you feel like the most interesting person in the room.

Above all, though, I've come to deeply respect Ryan's humility and vulnerability. He never lived his life in hopes of writing a book about it. And even though he's a gifted storyteller, Ryan's journey is not remarkable because of who he is. Instead, his journey (and in turn, this book) is remarkable because of *who God is*. My biggest credit to Ryan is how clearly he sees this truth, and how openly he shares his intensely personal and at times heartbreaking story—all in an effort to reveal God's awesome nature and abundant love.

Realer than Real is a book as multifaceted as its author: funny, insightful, tender, quirky, and—most importantly—God-glorifying.

—SCOTT DOBBE

To Kayla.

FOREWORD
By Tom Osborne

Realer Than Real is a story of the Wilkins' family struggles with personal tragedy which almost defies the probability that one family could endure so much trauma over a relatively short period of time. The book chronicles the tragic death of Kayla, the youngest daughter, in an auto accident at age 15, followed by an amazingly similar accident and injury suffered by an older daughter, Amber, and her very near brush with death and her struggle to recover. Amber reports being in the presence of Kayla while she is being transported to the hospital by life flight following her crash. This episode is similar to many reports of those involved with near-death experiences. All of this is told by the Wilkins' only son, Ryan, who chronicles these tragic events, the impact on the family, and the spiritual journey that ensues for all of the family members, including Ryan himself.

The book is well written, displays a remarkable willingness to be transparent and vulnerable to all aspects of personal struggle, grief, and suffering that the family endured, individually and collectively. The book illustrates the role that the family's strong Christian faith played in their struggles through all of the tragedy that they endured. Ryan writes very perceptively about each of his two sisters, their personalities, their endearing qualities, and some of the miraculous events that occurred throughout the family's ordeal. His account of the pain of his divorce and the role that faith played in his eventual healing and finding a person with a similar spiritual perspective is honest and instructive. *Realer Than Real* is a captivating story that any person of faith will find inspirational.

Realer than Real
A True Story of Grace, Hope, and Healing

For chapter-by-chapter photos, videos, and other resources, please visit:
www.RealerThanRealBook.com

CHAPTER 1

Saturday, August 25, 2001. The day was finally here: *Game*day. And not just any game, but my official Husker debut.

Like many Nebraska boys, I grew up playing backyard football and dreaming of the day when I'd put on the Big Red uniform. Now the wait was over.

Nebraskans love football the way scuba divers love air tanks: it's a relationship of necessity, and core to our basic functioning. The Cornhuskers have sold out every home game since 1962 and are the winningest team in college football during that span. When I was 12, 13, and 15 years old, my home state's team won the 1994, 1995, and 1997 National Championships. I pictured myself shucking tacklers like Tommie Frazier and throwing spirals like Brook Berringer. At an impressionable time in my life, the Huskers captured my heart.

The atmosphere was electric, as 77,473 fans—making Memorial Stadium the third-largest city in Nebraska at that moment—watched us congregate near the southwest corner of the end zone, pump-up music blaring, as we prepared to take the field for kickoff. I stood at the front of the pack. That morning, Coach told me I'd lead the charge onto the field. Scanning the stands, I breathed deeply and soaked in the roaring crowd before turning back to lock eyes with a few teammates, who were now bouncing feverishly as if spring-loaded and nodding their heads in anticipation. I stifled a cough, fearing that if I let it go, I might inadvertently release a butterfly from my stomach.

So much had led up to this, the first game of the 2001 season. The grueling two-a-day practices starting at 6 a.m. The punishing weightlifting regimen. The exhausting summer camps, where our squad worked tirelessly to perfect every drill so we knew we'd shine under pressure. The lingering aches and bruises, which required mental toughness to ignore, but which we knew were unavoidable parts of being a Husker.

It was time. I read Coach's lips as he pointed his finger toward the field: "LET'S GO!"

On cue, I raised my flag, emblazoned with the Big Red "N," and stormed onto the field with my fellow cheerleaders.

* * *

I had a terrific, and very blessed, childhood.

It wasn't always easy, though. My very first memory—I kid you not—is lying in my crib, face-down, squirming and screaming, as my mother fought to take my temperature—rectally. I was fifteen years old at the time. OK, I was probably two or three, but this memory still haunts me. Just try to make sense of that twisted act from a toddler's perspective. I vaguely remember wondering *"What is happening?!"* and *"Why am I being punished?!"* It was a simpler time, and I'm sure Mom thought she was doing the right thing, like the Medieval doctors who fought pneumonia with bloodletting leeches. The good news is things could only get better from there.

My father, Craig, grew up in a blue-collar neighborhood in South Omaha. His father was a mason tender (basically, a bricklayer's assistant) who typically worked two jobs and 70-hour workweeks to feed his family. The financial strain of my Dad's upbringing taught him three things: first, success required hard work and would not come easily; second, if at all possible, he needed a college degree; and third, he wanted to play a more active role in his children's lives than his father was able to play in his. These lessons motivated Dad to graduate from the University of Nebraska-Omaha in seven years (working full-time throughout college), achieve great success in banking, and become a loving, involved father.

2

When I was a child, Dad attended all of my sports games, helped me build my Cub Scout pinewood-derby car, taught me how to play chess, and entertained just about any other idea that interested me.

My mother, Shelly, was the youngest of three girls by about five minutes. She grew up in an Air Force family, and even though she moved around a lot during her childhood, she always had a steady pal in her twin sister, Kelly. Mom is kind-hearted, sensitive, and generous with her time. She'll do just about anything to help someone—anyone, even a stranger—and she always acts like it isn't the least bit inconvenient for her, even when it is. But to my Mom, *no one* is really a stranger; just a best friend in waiting. These days, I love this characteristic in her, but as a teenager it was a struggle. I would ask: "Mom, is it really important that your hairdresser knows I don't have a date to Homecoming?" Or: "Why did you tell our Applebee's waitress that Gizmo (our old dog) threw up in my ear?" The constant risk of embarrassment was a small price to pay for the gift of Mom, though, who stayed home to raise her children and sacrificed so much for us.

And then there was Amber, the first of my two younger sisters. Amber was born wearing a diamond-studded diaper and sporting a spray-tan. She texted before she could talk and sashayed before she could walk. Girly to the core, Amber was as foreign to me as a Chinese stereo manual. As far as I could tell, Amber was crazy about three things: shopping, ketchup (which she put on *everything*, even salad), and boys. Only the third category concerned me. An age-old riddle in my family was whether I innately disliked every guy Amber dated simply because I was her older brother, and that's what older brothers do (as my family maintained), or if I was fair and objective, and every guy Amber dated just happened to be a dud (as I claimed). In any case, as Amber's boyfriends grew progressively older, bigger, and more tattooed, my criticism became less vocal.

My youngest sister Kayla completed our family, both figuratively and literally. While Amber and I, at three years apart, went through typical sibling conflicts, Kayla—six years my younger—was just my kid sister who could do no wrong. Kayla loved animals and dreamt of becoming a veterinarian. One spring when she was about four years old, we discovered a litter of baby rabbits (called "kits") in a hole in our grandparents' backyard. We played with the kits all afternoon until a neighbor girl stopped by and informed us that because we had touched the babies with our "human hands," their mother would likely abandon or even eat them. We later learned this wasn't true, but not before Kayla had a good cry and begged my parents to "adopt" them. Besides loving animals, Kayla seemed to exist primarily to brighten the lives of others. One time, I came home from school feeling really down. I can't remember why, but I'll just guess it was one of three things: a girl I liked didn't like me back; I had a pimple; or a girl I liked didn't like me back *because* I had a pimple (double whammy!). As I laid face-down on my bed, trying not to cry, Kayla sat on the floor next to me, silently, and obviously feeling my pain. Then she left. That night, I discovered that Kayla had spent the next hour cleaning my car—a task I wouldn't wish on anyone. Kayla's tangible reminder that I was cared for immediately lifted my spirits. Even as a little girl, Kayla always had a knack for showing her great, selfless love through simple acts.

Growing up, my parents gave me a lot of freedom to be a boy. Our subdivision, Summerwood, was a typical American middle-income neighborhood. Most summer mornings, I'd wake up and yell to Mom, "I'm going to Brandon's!" and then disappear until dinnertime. My friends and I would play games like Tecmo Bowl, pickle, and Lighting Fireworks in Things. A long, sloped boulevard, which we kids just called "the ditch," stretched through the heart of Summerwood and was our playground. Some days, my friends and I would sneak through the ditch's keep-out bars, climb into a chosen sewage line, and just follow it until we saw daylight, where we would resurface and try to figure out where we were and how to get home.

As I progressed through middle school and into high school, insecurity set in. The source of my insecurity, I believe, was the tension between my desire to be perceived as extraordinary and my fear that, in reality, I might not be that special. I was good at a lot of sports, but not great at any of them. I was supposedly intelligent, according to teachers and standardized tests, but I didn't feel particularly smart, and I sometimes worried that I was an imposter. I was generally well-liked, but not all that popular.

In the summer before my senior year of high school, I begrudgingly (at my parents' insistence) joined my church's youth group for a weeklong mission trip to New York City. When you've regularly attended church since the day you were born, it's easy to go through the motions every Sunday without really growing, and that's where I had been for awhile. But on the mission trip, I recommitted my life to God—for the first time, in a way that felt personal and self-directed—and started to better understand the folly of measuring my worth by earthly standards, which could only lead to disappointment. That fall, I was baptized and grew closer to my new youth-group friends, who showed me faith and fun could mix. These developments helped lift from my shoulders the weight of anger and self-doubt I had been carrying, and freed me to be more joyful and authentic. And ironically, it wasn't until I loosened my grip on the world and refocused on God that the kinds of accolades I once so desperately chased after—in academics, leadership positions, and otherwise—started rolling in.

* * *

College was oodles of fun. One of my first orders of business when I arrived freshman year was to sign up to donate plasma—although it was more like a sale than a donation, because I made $50 a pop. I earmarked all proceeds as "date money." Each time I gave plasma, a nurse went through a checklist asking me whether, since my last visit, I had traveled to any one of a list of about 30 African countries considered to be at high risk for blood-borne diseases. Senegal?—No. Kenya?—No. Gabon?—No. Cameroon?—No. When the nurse got to the end of her checklist I would suddenly get a concerned look on my face and say, *"Wait—Did you say Gabon?!"* Then I would laugh and tell her that I was just kidding, I hadn't really visited Gabon. That joke never got old! (To me.)

The date money rolled in, but the dates didn't, so I decided to try out for cheerleading, where cute girls would *have* to hang out with me. Somehow I made the squad, but I was undoubtedly one of the least-talented guys on the team. Before one football game, ESPN cameras zoomed in on me and my female partner, who I proceeded to drop on live television during a stunting drill. I used to joke that you could always find me on the sidelines—just look for the guy standing next to the girl with crutches. As a rookie cheerleader, I also had some embarrassing mental lapses. One time, during a Nebraska-Kansas basketball game, the crowd was dead because we were losing by 20 points. So I picked up my megaphone and belted out a booming chant: "DEFENSE, HUSKERS, DEFENSE!" You guessed it: we were on offense. Another time, I ran the Husker flag onto the football field before the third quarter but forgot to first remove from my right pocket the full bottle of Gatorade I had stashed there during halftime. As I sprinted, my short red shorts sunk south, so I had to scuttle the length of the field with one hand holding the flag and the other holding up my pants. Cheerleading was a fun but humbling adventure.

During a social event my sophomore year, a friend and I started grumbling about the lameness of student government, and we decided that one of us should run for president. We flipped a coin, and I won. Thus, the "Boo Yah Party" was born. (Slogan: "We're not here to cheer 'ya . . . we're here to *Boo Yah!*") My total lack of student-government experience was received well from a jaded student body, and my running mates and I won the election handily. Once in office, we built some lasting achievements: we helped mount a successful student rally against the governor's proposed 10% university budget cut and implemented a popular Collegiate Readership Program (giving students cheap access to local and national newspapers), among other things. But the public light magnified my more embarrassing moments—like when our student government printed thousands of postcards for students to sign and mail to state senators reminding them to support the university so Nebraska's "best and bightest" students stayed in-state. After that debacle, I removed "attention to detail" from my resume.

The most impactful experience of my college career was counseling at Camp Kindle, a weeklong summer camp for children infected with or affected by HIV and AIDS. These children, who were battling through excruciating life circumstances at such tender ages, were precious and inspirational to me. Camp Kindle lets these kids be kids, just for a week. Campers learn they are not alone. For many, Camp Kindle is the only place where they can open up about how disease has impacted them. On the final night of camp, each child lit a candle and shared with the group one wish. I recall putting a hand over my eyes, quietly sobbing as a ten-year-old girl said, "I wish there were a cure for AIDS"; an eight-year-old boy said, "I wish camp could be all year"; and a six-year-old girl said, "I wish my mom was alive." In each of my two summers counseling, I learned much more from my campers than I taught them.

Throughout college, I forged lifelong friendships within my fraternity, FarmHouse—not to be confused with "Animal House." FarmHouse started in 1905 as a Bible study, and while the fraternity's faith-based roots remain woven into its traditions, today the organization has a more secular character. Entering college, I didn't see myself as a "frat guy" and was skeptical of the Greek system. But I liked most of the guys I met at FarmHouse and ultimately thought, *Why not, I've gotta live somewhere.* It's one of those decisions that I didn't put a lot of thought into but am tremendously grateful I made, as many of my closest friendships today were formed within FarmHouse's walls during my four years of college.

One of my favorite regular occurrences at FarmHouse was witnessing the power of "the Mob"—that is, the absurd antics that played out when a bunch of guys put their minds together toward mayhem. Like when the Mob busted into the room of my friend, Steve, wrestled him away from his girlfriend, carried him into the front yard, and saran-wrapped him to the flag pole for no reason whatsoever. The kicker came moments later, when Mob-member Scott decided to document the shenanigans by taking photos of Steve in his sad state, and then the Mob turned on Scott and saran-wrapped *him* to Steve. The Mob could be a fickle beast.

*   *   *

Around this time, I also got my first taste of the law—my future career field—when I defended myself in court against an ill-issued speeding ticket. The police had set up a speed trap on Vine Street—pointing their radar guns eastward into oncoming, campus-bound traffic—and were windmilling in hordes of unsuspecting drivers like me, seemingly arbitrarily, to park and await their citations. I was sure they had made a mistake—I wasn't speeding. Mine was the fifth car in a steady line of traffic; how, I wondered, could anyone distinguish my vehicle from the others as the column of cars approached the trap? But the ticketing officer insisted that from 857 feet away, and while I was in a 25 mile-per-hour school zone, he clocked me driving ten miles faster than the posted limit.

Stubborn and thirsty for justice, I refused to pay the fine. Instead, for the next month, I pored over books on traffic-ticket litigation and planned my defense. On my trial date, I arrived wearing my best (and only) suit—a black polyester ensemble from the Sears sales rack—and sweating profusely. The first step of successful defense, I had learned, was to show up; thousands of tickets are dismissed every year simply because the key testifying officer fails to appear. But I would have no such luck. My officer had already arrived and was glaring at me, obviously annoyed that I was making him jump through legal hoops. An ounce of anxiety-laden regret shot through me as I began to think: *This might not go well . . . like, at all.* But by then, the judge's bailiff was calling my case, and I took my seat alone at the defense table, nervously organizing my books, notepads, and accordion folders into neat piles while trying to take deep breaths and keep a leash on my fidgety legs. Without much delay, the State called their witness and the policeman started to testify, cued by the prosecuting attorney's friendly questions. I kept my head down and focused intently on my notes, waiting for the right time to spring my carefully prepared arguments.

"Objection!" I exclaimed, standing, when the officer first disclosed the model of his radar gun. "How do we know the witness is trained and competent to use this particular device?" As I spoke, I made wide, theatrical gestures with my arms, like all of the best attorneys I'd seen over the years in *Law & Order*. The police officer responded directly to the judge, meticulously ticking through his lofty credentials. As luck would have it, he was not only certified to use the radar gun, he had actually earned advanced certification and now *taught the radar-certification course* to rookie officers. Objection overruled. State 1, Ryan 0; I sat back down. A moment later, I struck out again: "Objection," I managed, now more sheepishly. "There is no evidence on the record establishing that the witness's radar gun was properly functioning on the date in question. If months or years had passed since the instrument's last calibration, the readings may not be accurate." This created a minor stir and slight headache for my opponents. The prosecutor asked for a short recess, and the testifying officer walked across the street to police headquarters to retrieve documentation verifying that his radar gun was tested and perfectly calibrated *the very morning* he cited me. "Overruled," the judge said again when we reconvened, now transparently embarrassed for me.

But I kept at it. As the officer went on, I spewed every conceivable objection my studies had mined, hoping something—anything—might stick. Using terms I barely understood like "hearsay," "best evidence," and "lacks foundation," I mucked up an impressive flurry of pointlessness. Then, finally, I landed a blow. During my cross examination of the officer, I noticed he was relying heavily on his handwritten notes and a copy of the citation to answer basic questions about the date, time, and other circumstances surrounding my alleged infraction. I addressed the judge: "Your honor, I request that you order the witness to put away his notes." I explained: "The Sixth Amendment guarantees me the right to confront my accusers. But the documents the officer is reading from aren't under oath, and I can't cross examine them. If the witness has no independent recollection of these events, he shouldn't be allowed to testify against me."

To this day, I have no idea whether my dramatic proclamation made any sense. But now the judge was fighting a smile, and—much to my astonishment—she agreed, allowing the officer a moment "to refresh his recollection," but ordering him to proceed without notes. Emboldened, I tested the officer's memory, peppering him with questions about weather conditions on the date of the incident. He stammered flimsy answers, now visibly less confident. Sensing he was on the ropes, I circled back to the core facts.

"Officer, what was the make and model of the car you clocked me driving?" After a long pause, he answered "I think it was a 1998 Honda Civic."

"You *think* it was a '98 Civic, or it _was_ a '98 Civic?" I asked.

"It _was_ a '98 Civic," the officer answered firmly.

Excitedly, I hoisted my copy of the citation toward the sky, exclaiming: "*In fact*, the citation you signed states I was driving a 1996 Toyota Camry! So which vehicle did you observe speeding—a '98 Civic or a '96 Camry?"

"A '96 Camry," the officer said, reversing course. He added, "Whichever car it was, I recognize you—you're the one I ticketed."

"But you didn't clock me *running* 35 miles per hour in a 25 mile-per-hour school zone," I reminded him. "You allegedly radared my car—which you just misidentified as a '98 Civic." "I have no more questions for this witness, your Honor," I said, triumphantly turning back toward the audience and finding no one.

Moments later, I took the stand to testify and offered the judge my exhibits, which consisted of enlarged color printouts of "the crime scene." The day after I got the ticket, I explained to the judge, my fraternity brother and I had returned to the exact location of the speed trap and measured out 857 feet, taking photos of approaching lines of traffic from that distance. Not surprisingly, it was near-impossible to distinguish one car from another.

All told, I put in a lot of time and effort to defend myself against a $60 ticket. But it was worth it in the end. Two weeks after the trial, the judge's decision arrived in the mail: not guilty.

*   *   *

Heading into my last week of college, life was looking good. I was set to graduate with a 4.0 grade-point average and had received the University's Outstanding Student Leadership Award, an honor bestowed on one male and one female each year for achieving the highest levels of community service and leadership. I also had a plan: Teach for America, a non-profit organization dedicated to eliminating educational inequality by enlisting top college graduates to teach in low-income communities. In a month, I would leave to teach summer school in Los Angeles before moving to St. Louis for my permanent placement teaching middle school that fall.

Finally, I had a partner: Beth, my fiancée, whom I would marry in three weeks. A vocal-music major and unapologetic ham, Beth beamed joy and big-heartedness. She greeted every homeless person on campus by name and knew many of their life stories. Few things made Beth happier than chatting about her family or dancing like a fool to pop-music hits at wedding receptions. On our first Valentine's Day as a couple, Beth snuck into my student-government office after-hours and streamed dozens of paper-cutout hearts from the ceiling, each one confessing a unique reason she loved me. Sometimes, Beth's happiness seemed so pure and radiant that it could lift everyone within a five-mile radius. As our college careers wound down together, I felt ever more grateful and excited to start my partnership with her. But our lives were about to change forever.

CHAPTER 2

"And Jesus replied, 'I assure you, today you will be with me in paradise.'"
—LUKE 23:43

On April 30, 2004, I turned 22 years old. As a gift, Beth let me watch the last five innings of the Cardinals-Cubs game from a sports bar in Iowa, and my beloved Cards gave me a win in the bottom of the ninth inning. We were in Iowa for our wedding shower thrown by Beth's family friends. Two days later—on Sunday, May 2—Beth and I drove back to Nebraska for our last week of finals. Beth was eager to get back to Lincoln because her next exam was on Monday, but my next test wasn't until Wednesday, so I was in no hurry. I decided to stay the night in Omaha.

Beth dropped me off at a McDonald's by the interstate, where Kayla—then 15, and armed with a learner's permit—picked me up in her gold Chevy Cavalier. Kayla was all smiles as I extended my hitchhiker's thumb and climbed into the backseat, behind my Mom. For years, I toted Kayla to church, the mall, and school, where I seldom passed up the opportunity to embarrass her in front of friends by honking maniacally and shouting "I LOVE YOU!" through the passenger-side window. Now, Kayla was clearly happy to be in the driver's seat. We made our way to a makeshift surprise birthday party for me at my parents' house; it was a surprise party in the sense that people yelled the word "SURPRISE!" when I arrived, but not a shocker in the sense that the guest list was comprised of the same extended family members I had celebrated every other birthday of my life with, and their cars were all parked out front.

The next day—Monday, May 3—was Kayla's show-choir finale. I had told Kayla I didn't think I could make it due to my finals schedule. But on the day of the event, for whatever reason—maybe I wanted to put off studying, or maybe I sensed it would mean a lot to Kayla—I changed my mind and decided to stick around Omaha for another night.

My family packed the house for Kayla's concert, and we enthusiastically applauded every tune. Kayla sang in the chorus; she was always more comfortable supporting than leading. But when I looked at her and focused, I could pick out her soft sweet voice. It was the same voice I'd heard practicing the same songs the night before, and a version of the same voice I had known and loved since the day Kayla was born. As I sat in the auditorium of Elkhorn High School watching my sister sing, I realized something else: my kid sister had become a beautiful young lady. I didn't know precisely when Kayla crossed the fine line separating childhood from young adulthood, but she had crossed it, and the boys were in trouble. After the performance, I waited with my family for Kayla to emerge from backstage. When she did, I responded by doing the two things that came most naturally to me: loving her and embarrassing her. I covered Kayla in a monster bear hug, kissed her cheeks, told her she sounded wonderful, wrapped her around my back— her legs curled in my left arm, and her shoulders and head in my right— and paraded her around the school, telling everyone she was my sister.

The next morning, Kayla woke up early for school. Before she left, she softly knocked on my bedroom door, opened it a few inches, and quietly said: "Ryan, thank you so much for coming to my show last night. Good luck with your finals—you will do great! I love you!" Half awake, I stayed in bed but murmured back: "Thanks, Kayla—I love you, too!" And those were the last words I ever said to my sister.

* * *

That evening—May 4, 2004—Kayla's best friend, Melanie, picked Kayla up on her way to their school's chapter of Youth for Christ, a faith-based student ministry that Kayla regularly attended. (By then, I was back in Lincoln studying for my upcoming final.) The guest speaker that night was a local businessman who shared his powerful testimony of how God's grace healed him in the wake of a painful childhood and saved him from a series of poor life choices he made as a teenager. At the conclusion of his talk, the group leader, Jason Currie, stood up and addressed the students. Jason's ministry style is relaxed and personable; he's not a "fire-and-brimstone" rabble-rouser. But that night, Jason's closing remarks took on a particularly solemn tone. Jason challenged the kids to "not wait" to get right with God, because "there's no guarantee what tomorrow will look like, or if we will even have a tomorrow." Life is fragile, and faith is too important to postpone.

Jason closed in prayer and dismissed the kids around 8:30 p.m. Kayla and Melanie filed out with a third friend, Nick, who had asked Melanie for a ride home. As the group departed, Jason wished them a good week and told Kayla, "See you later."

*　*　*

At 8:50 p.m., Mom got the call. She was lying on the couch watching TV in the living room. Dad was nearby in the kitchen, preparing for the next day's work meeting.

"Hello?" Dad's attention shifted to Mom as tense silent seconds followed.

"Is she OK?" More waiting. " . . . Where?"

Mom hung up the phone and bolted for the garage, forcing just one word: "*Hurry.*"

*　*　*

As they jumped in their car and headed to the scene, Mom and Dad didn't know much—Kayla was in a car accident, it sounded serious, and emergency services were responding. Due to a misunderstanding, my parents initially drove to the wrong intersection and lost precious, frantic minutes unraveling their confusion and rerouting their course. As Dad drove west on Center toward 222nd Street—a dark, hilly, winding stretch of road in the far outskirts of Omaha—the landscape looked more or less normal, belying what lay ahead. Then the road made its final curve, and reality unfolded: a burst of flashing lights and a sea of police officers, firefighters, and medical responders.

A fire truck blocked my parents' path a couple hundred feet from the accident. Dad parked and sprinted forward, where three firefighters converged on him. "You don't understand," Dad said, "I think my daughter was involved in this accident." As he spoke, Dad looked over the firefighter's shoulder to see, for the first time, a parked helicopter waiting to rush an unknown victim to the University of Nebraska Medical Center, 17 miles away. The firefighters told Dad they could not let him pass, but they pointed out a side road he might take for an alternate access point. Dad rushed back to the car, drove to where the firefighters had signaled, and then approached the intersection on foot again, this time from the north. Two deputy sheriffs again told Dad he could not pass, but they allowed him to press between them. In the commotion, Dad overlooked the scene to his far right, where a sheet was placed over the body of Kayla's friend, Nick, who had just been pronounced dead.

Dad stood in the middle of the intersection, where a few confused seconds passed like an eternity. He saw Melanie sitting near the road, sobbing but apparently uninjured as Jason, the Youth for Christ campus leader, tried to console her. *But where was Kayla?* Suddenly, a team of EMTs charged toward Dad, who was standing between them and the helicopter. As the medical crew passed, wheeling a gurney, Dad saw the devastating sight that will be forever etched in his memory: his youngest child, Kayla, with a mouthful of tubes and a visible right head wound that had bloodied her blonde hair. Dad chased the medics to the helicopter, but he could not fly with them; all available space was dedicated to Kayla and the emergency team.

Dad ran back toward his car, where Mom was waiting with the deputy sheriffs. By now, a crowd of concerned kids and parents had gathered around the police perimeter. A family friend offered to take my parents to the hospital, insisting they were in no shape to drive. My parents agreed, and Dad called me.

*　*　*

Actually, Dad called 411. In his hurried state, he had rushed out of the house without his cell phone, and he did not know my number by heart. So using his friend's phone, Dad called information, asked to be routed to FarmHouse's main line in Lincoln, and explained to a fraternity brother that my sister had been in a car accident, she was being life-flighted to the Med Center, and I needed to come quickly.

My fraternity brother found me in my room and gave me the news. As I listened, a chill ran over my entire body, from the top of my spine down through my toes and fingertips. "Which sister?" I asked, numbly. He did not know. I reached Dad on his friend's phone and learned it was Kayla. Then I called Beth and asked her to pick me up and take me to Omaha. As I waited for her, I walked down the hall to FarmHouse's "Blue Room," where two close friends lived. I stood in their doorway in a stunned stupor and said: "Kayla was in a terrible accident. She might die. *I am so, so scared.*" I fell onto my knees, and then face-down onto the floor, crying profusely. My friends put their hands on my shoulders and prayed.

*　*　*

One hour from Lincoln to Omaha, but so much longer. I alternated between moments of composure—where Beth and I prayed for Kayla and reminded ourselves she was alive at the scene and with skilled doctors now—and fits of overwhelming fear and despair, where I struggled to breathe and rocked back and forth in my seat repeating, over and over, "Oh God" and "please no." I discovered muscles in my face that I didn't know existed. They were tight and pained, awoken by the drastic straining from my sudden facial contortions.

Meanwhile, my parents arrived at the ER's waiting room. Besides Kayla's accident, it must have been a quiet night in Omaha, because no one was there. Mom and Dad were escorted to a private, separate waiting room, where they waited for news on Kayla's condition. The minutes passed: 10, 20, 30. Mom sat quietly; Dad paced. A nurse popped in and said they were still working to stabilize Kayla, and to keep waiting. At

16

one point, Dad peeked back into the main waiting area and was taken aback by what he saw: the recently barren room was now packed with Kayla's classmates and our friends and family. They filled every chair and the standing area, and they lined the walkway leading toward the hospital entrance.

From the private waiting room, Dad could see through a window into the hospital's main medical hub. He saw our family physician, who had reported to the hospital immediately after he learned of the accident. Dad searched his face for clues about Kayla's prognosis. The doctor looked up from his notes and glanced toward my parents' private waiting room and met eyes with Dad. The men held their glances for a second or two, and then the doctor lowered his eyes, grimaced, and sadly shook his head, telegraphing the message he could not yet verbalize.

Minutes later, the head of the emergency room entered my parents' private waiting area with a nurse. There were three chairs in the room. Dad sat in one, Mom sat to Dad's right, and the doctor sat across from both of them, with the nurse standing in the corner. The doctor explained Kayla's condition: severe traumatic brain injury caused by an external impact to the right side of Kayla's head. Her brain was swelling, but her skull constricted the brain's available space, creating tremendous pressure within Kayla's cranium. Mom took all of this in, and then asked the only question that really mattered: "Is she going to be OK?" The doctor hesitated, then answered: "We are doing everything we can . . . but it does not look good."

Mom went limp, slumped into her chair, and rolled onto the ground in one motion. She had fainted. The nurse propped Mom up as the doctor opened the door to the medical hub and yelled, "Code Blue!" Now it was Mom's turn to be lifted onto a gurney and wheeled away wearing an oxygen mask. Mom's medical team inserted an IV into her wrist and pumped Valium into her bloodstream, which put her in a restful state for the next few hours. Now Dad sat alone, his wife and youngest child in separate hospital rooms, and Amber and I still en route in separate cars. Finally, a nurse arrived to escort him to Kayla.

As Dad entered the room and looked down upon his daughter, he saw she still looked like . . . Kayla. Her eyes were closed, her head wrapped in gauze, and her skin paler and puffier, but her face and body were mostly unblemished, with just a few cuts and bruises. A machine controlled Kayla's breathing, forcing oxygen into her lungs, and a bevy of gadgets measured Kayla's vital signs. Dad's eyes shifted to Kayla's IV, where liquid drugs dripped into Kayla's veins at an alarming rate; instead of the usual slow, pronounced drip, Kayla's IV streamed a steady trickle.

"What is she getting?" Dad asked a nearby nurse.

"A painkiller," the nurse responded.

"Can you give her any more?" Dad inquired. "I don't want her to be in pain."

"I'm sorry, Mr. Wilkins," the nurse answered, "but her current dosage already far exceeds the maximum recommended guideline."

Dad read between the lines: Kayla's medical team had shifted their focus from saving her life to keeping her comfortable in her final hours.

Kayla's neurologist then spoke with Dad to shed additional light on her state. When the brain swells in the wake of a traumatic impact, the neurologist said, the patient's fate is sealed when her intracranial pressure becomes so great that her brainstem—the region that connects the brain to the spinal cord—"blows out," like a cork from a wine bottle. Dad asked the question that he didn't want answered: "Has that happened?" The neurologist's tone was sympathetic but firm: "Yes."

*   *   *

Beth and I reached the hospital around 10 p.m. By then, Amber had also arrived. When I saw my little sister lying in that bed, it was hard to know what to do. A part of me wanted to curl up next to Kayla and pour out my emotion, telling her I loved her, we all needed her, and she could not die. But my protective impulse was stronger, and I determined that, to the extent Kayla had any level of perception (conscious or unconscious), she was probably very scared, and I needed to comfort her. For me, this meant two things.

First, I was never going to let go of Kayla's right hand. As long as she breathed, her hand would be touched, caressed, and gripped. As long as Kayla could feel, she would feel my warmth and safety. She would know I was there and that she was not alone. If I had to briefly leave the room to use the restroom or get a glass of water, I would put another person's hand into Kayla's in place of mine and then resume my duties as soon as I returned.

Second, my family and I were going to talk to her, calmly but constantly. If Kayla could hear anything, it wasn't going to be silence, crying, or mechanical beeps, but rather the steady voice of the people she loved and trusted most. Sometimes, I gave Kayla words of assurance: "Kayla, you look really good. Your heart rate is steady. We cannot wait to see you open your eyes!" I tried not to say anything that would suggest to Kayla that we questioned whether she would survive. Like the rest of my family, I also shared words of love, reminding Kayla how much I adored her, how much joy she brought to my life, and how excited I was to continue to watch her grow.

Outwardly, I was cool and even-keeled for the most part. But on the inside, I felt sick. For Kayla's entire life, as her big brother, I was her protector. When she was bullied, I searched out her bully; when she was sad, I cheered her up; when she fell and skinned her knee, I picked her up and carried her home. Now, when she needed me most—when her life depended on it—I felt useless.

As the hours passed, I talked to Kayla about memories of happier times. I reminded her of a past Christmas Eve, when she was five years old and adamant about staying up late to greet Santa and his reindeer with milk and cookies. When Mom and Dad checked in on her that night, Kayla closed her eyes and pretended to be asleep. Moments later, Kayla heard footsteps downstairs—could it be? *Santa?!* Kayla tiptoed down the stairs and craned her neck toward the Christmas tree in our living room. A minute later, she was in my doorway looking shaken and defeated. "Ryan ... why are Mom and Dad putting presents under the tree?" "Oh, Beaner!" I answered, using the nickname I gave Kayla when she was a toddler. "Let's go talk to Mom and Dad about it." I held Kayla's hand

and led her back downstairs, where we ambushed our parents. The jig was up, and they came clean. By the next morning, Kayla was fine—it helped when she learned that she didn't need Santa to get most of the toys on her wish list.

I talked with Kayla about cheerleading—our unlikely shared interest. If you had told my parents in 1990 that one of their kids would grow up to be a college cheerleader, they would have secretly prayed it wasn't me. But Kayla was one of a few people who definitely thought it was cool that her big brother cheered for Nebraska. Kayla and I did not have many hobbies in common, and cheerleading gave us a wonderful, unexpected way to bond. When Kayla tried out for her school's cheer squad at the end of her freshman year, I coached her on proper techniques, showing her how to "punch" her cheer motions with sharp, snappy movements: arms stiff, wrists straight, muscles tight. I felt like Mr. Miyagi teaching my obedient Kayla-san. We practiced "walk-in" stunting together—the drill where I squatted and she stepped toward me, planted her right foot in my hands, and I hoisted her up while spinning her 180 degrees, with the end result of Kayla standing atop my hands, looking forward, at my shoulder height. One of the happiest smiles I ever saw on Kayla's face came the day she found out she made her school's varsity squad. It was a Saturday, and Kayla had been a nervous wreck since completing tryouts that morning. Suddenly, three senior cheerleaders pulled up in our driveway. I met them at the front door: "Are you here for Kayla? Come on in! She's on the pot but will be right out." A mortified Kayla yelled "RYAN!" from her room on the second floor, but when she looked down the stairs to see her new fellow cheerleaders smiling up at her with fists full of congratulatory balloons and streamers, she lit up with joy. Today, I am so thankful for my improbable cheerleading connection with Kayla, which blessed me with these beautiful memories.

It's normal for a little sister to be proud of her big brother. But as I sat by Kayla's side, holding her hand and reminiscing as the hours passed into the early morning of May 5, I recognized something: I was so proud of her, too. Not for her achievements and accolades, but for her gentle spirit and humble character, which are much rarer and harder to attain.

Kayla loved and cared for others unconditionally and relentlessly. Kayla forgave others when they didn't ask for her forgiveness. Kayla, I realized for perhaps the first time, was *one of the best people I knew*. Her injuries were so sudden, so harsh, and it pained me to think I might never have another conversation with her. I'd never get another opportunity to tell her how much I loved and admired her. I could not fathom this finality. While Dad, Mom (who had by this time rejoined us), and Amber shared their own dear memories with Kayla, I lowered my head and prayed for a miracle. "God, please save my sister. Nothing is impossible for you. God, I believe you *can* do this, and I know you *want* to do this because you love Kayla and she loves serving you. So please, God, let Kayla live."

Despite my prayers, Kayla's heart rate slowly but steadily declined throughout the night: 100 beats per minute around 10 p.m., 80 beats per minute by midnight, and 50 beats per minute by 4 a.m. By 7 a.m., Kayla's heartbeat was faltering considerably and fluttering below 30 beats per minute. The monitors beeped and whirred, recording her decline, and it seemed that any breath could be Kayla's last. Amber stood near the foot of Kayla's bed in a sort of a daze. (Years later, Amber told me she was barely able to take in what was happening, and that she had very little recollection of these events.) In these final minutes, Mom softly caressed Kayla's leg, quietly repeating "please, my baby, please." Dad kissed Kayla's knees and the area around her eyelids, hoping these sensitive spots could still feel his lips. And I leaned in toward Kayla's ear and told her another story.

When Kayla was nine years old, my family bought a piano, and Kayla started taking lessons. She loved the fact that no one else in our family played the instrument—it was her "thing." But after school one day, Kayla came home to find *me* playing *her* piano. I was bumbling through the tune of "You Are My Sunshine," plunking it out by ear. Once I had it down, I scribbled the melody onto a piece of sheet music paper and stashed it under the piano bench alongside Kayla's lesson books. Days later, I was pleased to hear Kayla practicing the song—presumably aided by my notes! But as I walked closer and looked over Kayla's shoulder,

I saw a different document, this one in Kayla's handwriting, and labeled "You Are My Sunshine—by Kayla Wilkins." That stinker had copied my notes onto a fresh sheet of paper, wrote her name on the new product, and destroyed the original! Apparently, this was Kayla's way of marking her territory. From then on, I respected the piano as Kayla's domain.

Smiling and crying, I shared this final memory with Kayla, telling her "Kayla, you *are* our sunshine! You brighten our lives every day!" Then my parents pointed out a surprising observation: as I spoke, Kayla's heartbeat rebounded. In fact, for the first time since we arrived at the hospital, Kayla's heart rate was trending up, not down. Seizing on this progress and still praying for her survival, I kissed Kayla's cheeks, told her we were still with her, and began to sing:

> You are my sunshine,
> My only sunshine!
> You make me hap-*py*!
> When skies are gray.
> You'll never know, dear,
> How much I love you.
> Please don't take my sunshine away.

Amber joined me, and together we repeated the song's chorus over and again as Kayla's heart continued its brilliant ascent toward 60 beats per minute, then 90 beats per minute, eventually reaching 117 beats per minute. For a moment, it appeared we were all about to witness a modern-day miracle—God plucking his child from the grips of death and using her recovery to demonstrate his awesome power and love for us.

But that's not what happened. As quickly as it had risen, Kayla's heart rate plateaued and then rapidly retreated. Afterward, a Christian doctor told my family he believes that when a patient's heartbeat soars during her final moments, this is her soul being summoned to heaven; or perhaps the patient's first glimpse—from a perspective beyond our understanding—of the glory of God. Within minutes, Kayla's heart gave back all of the progress it had made. I held Kayla's cool, clammy hand as long pauses passed between light heartbeats. It had been more than ten hours since Kayla's accident, and her body could not fight any longer. Silently, I asked God to protect my sister so she would not be scared, and to let Kayla know that we loved her and would miss her, but she could go. Finally, around 8:15 a.m., Kayla's heart took its last beat. And I faced the sickening reality that, to this day, is still very difficult for me to accept. My little sister was dead.

CHAPTER 3

"I love those who love me, and those who seek me find me."
—PROVERBS 8:17

When the doctors pronounced Kayla dead, my Mom began to cough and wheeze, struggling to breathe, and then she fainted—again. She was taken to a separate room for another round of Valium. Then, with harsh but necessary speed, a doctor pulled Dad into the hallway and asked him to consider donating Kayla's organs to others in need of transplants. Dad was dumbfounded; he never thought he'd have to answer this question on his child's behalf. He asked me what I thought we should do. It was at once the hardest and easiest decision I've faced. Hard because it pained me to think of my sister's body enduring postmortem operations; easy because there was no question in my mind that, if faced with the choice, Kayla would choose to give—so that's what we did. Weeks later, we were comforted when we found Kayla's learner's permit in her Chevy Cavalier. Under the word "DONOR" was a red heart encircling the letter "Y" for yes. Sure enough, Kayla wanted to be an organ donor.

It was a strange thing, saying goodbye to Kayla. Her body was there, but she wasn't. I crawled into Kayla's bed and lay by her side, no longer concerned about disrupting her medical equipment. I held Kayla to my chest, crying, and told her I would try to honor her life with mine, part of me talking to the body in my arms, and part of me lifting a prayer to her in heaven. Then it was time for us to go. To save as much tissue and as many organs as possible, the surgeons needed to act quickly. In a gesture that failed to capture the surreality of the moment, we kissed Kayla farewell and, finally, left her.

*   *   *

Emotionally drained and without sleep for more than a day, the next several hours were a blur. Beth drove me toward my parents' home, and on the way we took a detour to Kayla's accident site. The intersection was already so well-cleared of debris that I couldn't tell exactly where the crash occurred. Later, I learned a little more about the accident: on the way home from Youth for Christ, Melanie accelerated northbound from a stop sign without seeing the westbound pickup truck bearing down on her at 55-60 miles per hour. The pickup driver did not (or could not) brake, and the unconstrained impact crushed the passenger's side (that is, Kayla's side), tossing Kayla and Nick from Melanie's car.

At my parents' house, I tried to sleep, unsuccessfully. The muscular pain my face felt from wrenching and sobbing the night before had by now shifted to a dull numbness covering my lower cheeks through my forehead, as if I had received a Novocain facial. When I closed my eyes, my mind stirred with painful thoughts about Kayla's injuries and her last moments, and from time to time I was gripped by new implications of her death: I would never see Kayla graduate from college, or fall in love and get married, or become a mother; my future children would never know their aunt; more immediately, Kayla would not be a bridesmaid in my wedding at the end of the month.

Another reality: I would never, ever make a new memory with Kayla. And its corollary: my finite, existing memories of Kayla were the only ones I would ever have, and when I lost those memories, they (and in a way, my sister) would be gone forever. I grabbed a pen and paper and racked my brain for memories, hoping that Kayla's life and legacy might feel more permanent if I could capture them in writing. I recalled Kayla as a sixth-grader, when she puzzlingly became a diehard Packers fan right around the time she developed a crush on a boy from church who also just happened to like the team. Kayla successfully pleaded with my Mom to buy her a Packers jacket she found at a post-winter clearance sale. It was three sizes too big, but she wore it all the time—even that summer. Kayla proudly told whoever would listen that her favorite player was the Green Bay quarterback, "Brett Fav-ree."

I remembered baking Jell-O cookies with Kayla on our last Christmas Eve together, and eating half the dough before we got anything in the oven. I remembered sitting on a blanket with Kayla at the top of our home's second-floor stairs, when I was about nine and she was about three, and holding Kayla tight as I piloted us downward, our tailbones thudding and our excited yells breaking with every step.

I thought about Kayla's 15th birthday—her last. As usual, our entire extended family was on hand. Kayla's gift from my parents that year was her first cell phone, and Mom and Dad asked me to devise a clever way to give it to her. I thought I'd make Kayla work for it, so I wrote a series of clues that sent Kayla scurrying all over our house to find her present. Clue #1 told Kayla to look under a "feather-filled object in the dirtiest room in the house." Quicker than I liked, Kayla deduced that her next clue was in my bedroom, under my pillow. Kayla found it and read Clue #2 aloud: "If you find the next clue, you'll be getting warmer." Kayla checked the fireplace first—good idea, but no dice. Then she ran to the kitchen, where she found her next clue in the oven. (In retrospect, hiding a paper clue in the oven wasn't my brightest idea.) Kayla excitedly read Clue #3: "You'll find the next clue on a game board in the second-largest room in the house." After a momentary pause, Kayla bounded upstairs to my parents' closet—which was, in fact, the second-biggest room in our house, an absurdity not lost on us kids—where she found her fourth clue atop Dad's chess board. That clue told Kayla to grab a nearby cordless phone and proceed to her final clue, which was "being held captive by the King of the Jungle"—a lion perched on the floor of my parents' safari-themed basement.

Kayla raced downstairs, out of breath—by my design, she had by then scaled nine flights of stairs in just a few minutes—and collected her last clue, which instructed her to call a phone number using our landline and listen. She dutifully obeyed, and seconds later, her shiny new cell phone erupted ... from the sleeve of my shirt. Kayla burst out laughing with her sweet, genuine smile—the kind that spread so wide it made her eyes close—and pulled her birthday gift from my sleeve, along with one last note. This one was more sentimental than instructional: "Use this phone to call your brother!" Kayla smiled again for the family camera, and then looked back at me: "I will!"

In these precious memories, Kayla lived. I collected and clung to them like treasures. I searched for photos, gifts we had exchanged over the years, and other artifacts evidencing that Kayla loved me, and that she knew I loved her. In Kayla's room, I found a diary-like book which, based on her handwriting, I suspected Kayla worked through when she was about twelve years old. The book had various leads and cues for Kayla to complete, like "My favorite food is . . . " or "My biggest pet peeve is . . . " One page had an illustration of a brain divided into a number of compartments, which Kayla filled in to depict what was literally "on her mind." She must have been writing during the summer, because across one brain section she simply wrote "AIR CONDITIONING." She labeled another part "Green Bay Packers" and another "Tobey"—our family's Shih Tzu puppy, and one of Kayla's best friends. But tucked in the bottom-right corner was the piece of Kayla's mind that made my heart soar: "Ryan Wilkins." I cherished the confirmation that I had been on my sister's mind.

I found Kayla's "Precious Moments" Bible, which she had read since grade school, and flipped backwards through the gospels, paying closest attention to excerpts Kayla had marked with handwritten notes. There was Luke 12:40, which Kayla had highlighted in yellow: "You must also be ready, because the Son of Man will come at an hour when you do not expect him." How strange, I thought, that Kayla, as a young, healthy teenager, honed in on a verse that reminded her to live her life in such a way that she was "ready" for Jesus at any time. Then there was Matthew 18, where Kayla starred and bracketed the following passage:

At that time the disciples came to Jesus and asked, "Who, then, is the greatest in the kingdom of heaven?"

He called a little child to him, and placed the child among them. And he said: "Truly I tell you, unless you change and become like little children, you will never enter the kingdom of heaven. Therefore, whoever takes the lowly position of this child is the greatest in the kingdom of heaven. And whoever welcomes one such child in my name welcomes me."

Nearby, Kayla wrote: "God 1st. Others 2nd. Me last." Reading this, I choked up again, realizing how simply but perfectly it captured how Kayla lived her life—serving God by serving others, and submitting her will to his. I smiled with hope in Jesus' promise that my selfless sister might now be among the "greatest in the kingdom of heaven." And my smile turned to laughter when I scanned to Matthew 18:15-16, on the next page of Kayla's Bible, where I found another passage, bracketed and *double* starred, and titled "Dealing with a Sinning Brother."

In Kayla's TV/VCR combo was a video recording of the 4th Annual "Mr. Millard West" competition—my former high school's faux-beauty pageant for men, which I won my senior year. Typically, the crown goes to the contestant who best makes a fool of himself during each phase of the competition, and my year was no different. Kayla kept the recording on standby in her room, always ready to show it off to visiting friends or sneak in a late-night giggle.

In the last few years of Kayla's life, I was so busy with college. When she died, I desperately wished I would have called her more; that I would have told her more often and more sincerely that I loved her and I was proud of her; that I would have been more deliberately involved in *Kayla's* life, and not just indirectly by virtue of us both being present at the same family events. I knew I had been a good brother to Kayla, but I wished I had been better. And now it was too late to do anything about it. Kayla's diary, her Mr. Millard West recording, and other keepsakes—silly as some were—gave me precious assurance of our mutual love when I needed it most.

*   *   *

Around 10 p.m. that night—almost fourteen hours after Kayla passed away—I sat on my porch with Beth and Scott, who had driven up from FarmHouse in Lincoln to see me. I began to process some feelings out loud. In time, I told Beth and Scott, I could learn to accept that Kayla was gone—if only God could somehow assure me that she was with him. *With him . . . where?* I realized that I had never before seriously contemplated heaven. The whole concept was like a cartoon to me—with fluffy clouds, pearly gates, and singing angels. Now, reality mattered— really, *where is my sister? Is heaven real?* Or is Kayla just . . . *gone?* That cold fate I could not accept. I told Beth and Scott that I wasn't mad at God for what happened to Kayla. I didn't think it was fair for me to demand that God insulate me and my family from pain and loss. But I *didn't* think it was too much to ask God to give me a sign that my sister's spirit lived on, intact, though perhaps in a way I couldn't understand. And that sign, that reassurance, is what we prayed for together on the porch that night.

It was time to change gears: "Who's up for a chocolate shake?" I asked, desperate for a pick-me-up. We climbed into Scott's truck and headed to Burger King. When we got there, it was 10:55 p.m. and the restaurant had just closed—five minutes early! On our way back home, I asked Scott to drive to Kayla's crash site again. There was no particular reason to go; I had been there earlier in the day, and now it was late and quite dark. But I felt compelled to return.

When we arrived, we found that in the hours since Beth and I first visited the intersection that morning, dozens of Nick and Kayla's friends had canvassed the area with signs, stuffed animals, and personal mementos. Two tall white crosses stood near the intersection with a marker attached so people could share memories or write notes to them. While Beth wrote on Kayla's cross and Scott stood nearby, I lay down in the grass by myself. This was a place where I felt close to Kayla—closest to where her heart last beat and her lungs last breathed without help. I thought about my sister and wondered where she was, right then. Could she see me crying? Could she hear me calling out to her? I prayed to God for Kayla's presence, and for his peace and assurance.

After a few minutes, I rejoined Scott and Beth as we got ready to head home. It was around midnight, and a full moon lit the sky. We stood together in a circle, silently, heads down, with the cool spring breeze rolling through the open fields and brushing our cheeks. Then, like a whisper, a faint hum faded in and out of earshot. The sound went virtually unnoticed. Scott and I looked up and met eyes, but neither of us reacted outwardly. The humming stopped momentarily, and then it returned. The sound was quiet and muffled, but unmistakable: a ringing phone. Still, no one reacted. Scott thought it was Beth's phone; Beth and I thought it was Scott's phone. But by the end of the second set of rings, it sunk in—*that's not our phone.* We stood *en garde* like statues, still as we could be, listening. Beth prayerfully pleaded aloud: "Please, let it ring again!" Almost on cue, the third set of ringing commenced, and I plunged toward the sound into a thatch of tall grass and thick weeds, intently concentrating as I drew ever closer, but again the ringing ceased before I could pinpoint its source. We all looked at each other silently and a bit frantically, waiting and wishing we could hear the ring one more time. None of us knew precisely what—whose phone—we were looking for, but the air was heavy with significance. A moment later it came: the fourth and final ring. I fell to my knees in the dense brush, desperately pawing at the dirt and ripping at grass, where I finally found it: a half-buried cell phone. I flipped the phone open and read the screen: "Ricky Loves You."

In a flash, it dawned on me: Ricky was Kayla's boyfriend. The phone was Kayla's. A rush of peace and joy overwhelmed me as I fell forward onto my hands and cried out to God in thanks. *He gave me the sign!* I felt God had answered my prayer, miraculously. What other word could describe it? Kayla's phone survived a high-impact collision that took two lives and totaled as many vehicles. Police cars, fire trucks, ambulances, a helicopter, and emergency personnel had all trampled the crash site without disturbing the phone. All debris was thoroughly scrubbed from the site that morning, and dozens of Kayla's friends and classmates had visited the site that afternoon, but the phone remained unharmed and undetected. I checked the phone's call history and found that four—and only four—calls were made in the thirty minutes before and after we found the phone. We needed all four calls to find it. (The calls came from Kayla's friends, who later told me they just felt compelled to listen to Kayla's voicemail greeting at that moment.) We also needed Burger King to close early; a spring day without rain (it stormed later that evening); a cell-phone battery with life (*at least* 30 hours had passed since Kayla's last-possible recharge); and a loud ringer setting. Reflecting on this night years later, Scott summed it up well: "I just remember the feeling that we were lost that evening, all of us in some sort of shock, and out driving for no particular reason other than we felt the need to step away from the house. And so later, after finding Kayla's phone, I was struck by the apparent randomness of the trip. Which is to say of course that it wasn't random at all."

I have always been skeptical of claimed miracles and so-called signs from God; by my nature, I rely more on evidence than on feelings. But in this case, I simply believed that the most logical explanation was that God had answered my prayers by giving me a sign that Kayla was in his care. His delivery was beautiful: From the site that brought on Kayla's death, God offered proof of her life. Just like I had sent Kayla on a goose chase to find her birthday gift months before, God now watched me run, scuttle, and dig to find the same cell phone, which was now his gift to me. And by using Kayla's phone to answer my prayers, God helped Kayla deliver on her 15th-birthday promise to me: "*Use this phone to call your brother!*"

* * *

That night, I set the alarm clock on Kayla's cell phone for 8:15 a.m.—exactly 24 hours after she passed away. I wanted to wake up, pray, and think about my sister and what God had done for me on this one-day anniversary. I finally zonked out on the living-room floor around 1 a.m. It was my first meaningful sleep in more than 40 hours. But the next morning, I woke up on my own. Kayla's cell phone was gone; Dad had picked it up early that morning when he saw it on the floor by my head. My heart sunk. I had really wanted to acknowledge that moment, and I was certain I had slept in too late and missed my chance. Then I walked into the kitchen and saw the microwave clock: 8:14 a.m. (and running one minute slower than Kayla's cell-phone clock, I later learned). I hadn't missed my opportunity to thank God and memorialize that moment after all.

Kayla's funeral at Christ Community Church a few days later was a celebration of her life. Scores of people touched by Kayla's spirit and story packed the pews and lined the balcony, maxing out the building's 2,200-seat capacity in what the former head pastor described as the largest memorial service the church had ever held. Several vans made multiple trips to transport the 104 floral arrangements decorating Kayla's service. The Elkhorn High School choir—which Kayla had performed with just days before—filled the stage and sang, wearing bright colors.

Even though we thanked God throughout the service for the gift of Kayla's life, we could not deny our deep pain. My spirit was heavy and drained; I channeled what little energy I had into accepting condolences on my family's behalf and putting a poised face on our inestimable grief. Somehow, Mom mustered the courage to sing a song called "Goodbye for Now," a poignant tribute to Kayla which perfectly captured the tension between our hope and heartache:

> I can't believe that you're really gone now
> Seems like it's all just a dream
> How can it be that the world will go on
> When something has died within me?
>
> Leaves will turn, my heart will burn with colors of you
> Snow will fall but I'll recall your warmth
> Summer wind breathing in your memory
> I'll miss you
>
> . . .

On rainy days, in many ways, you'll water my heart
On starry nights I'll glimpse the light of your smile
Never far from my heart you'll stay with me
So I'll just wait

'Cause there will be a time when I'll see your face
And I'll hear your voice and there we will laugh again
And there will come a day when I'll hold you close
No more tears to cry 'cause we'll have forever
But I'll say goodbye for now

My family and I experienced numerous other blessings in the months that followed. Many came in the form of friends and complete strangers, in the Omaha community and from afar, whom God used to wrap us in love and understanding. For weeks, family friends answered our phones, fed us, wrote and mailed thank-you notes on our behalf, and took initiative to lighten our burdens. Other parents who lost their children in years past wrote to Mom and Dad with nuggets of wisdom on how they coped. Kayla's friends and classmates regularly popped by to delight us with new accounts of Kayla's sweet nature. One boy visited our home with his mother and described how he had long felt like an outcast at school, but he always looked forward to homeroom, where Kayla would smile at him, tell him "good morning," and ask him how he was doing. This small effort, he said, made all the difference some days. Another girl told us how money was tight in her home, and this was an embarrassing issue for her and her family. From time to time, she went to school without lunch money. Quietly and casually, Kayla shared her lunch with this girl or, in some instances, just gave the girl her lunch money, insisting (half-convincingly) that she "wasn't hungry anyhow."

And precious stories like these just kept trickling in. *Six years* after Kayla's passing, a young woman blessed us with this account:

> I went to school with Kayla. I sat at her lunch table
> and she was one of the sweetest girls I ever met. I

remember everyday before lunch she would pray . . . I never thought much of this, but now that I am older I think, "Wow, how brave she must have been to do that in front of everyone; that is, to show her faith like that."

One day in gym class our lockers were right next to each other, and I had forgotten my gym shoes. I was actually wearing flip flops at the time. I mentioned to Kayla how scared I was because I was going to get into trouble. She offered me her gym shoes. I figured she must have had an extra pair.

A few minutes later, after I was already out on the gym floor, Kayla walked in fully clothed in gym clothes EXCEPT that she was wearing the white sandals she had worn to school that day! I was stunned that she would give me her only gym shoes and risk herself getting into trouble. I was so touched by this and knew Kayla was different from the rest of us; she was special.

Kayla was so special to me ever since that day. And thanks to Kayla, I don't care if people see me pray.

Time and again, we were touched by two of Kayla's favorite subjects—music and animals—which we believe God used to cover us with his peace and Kayla's spirit during particularly difficult moments. For example, there was the time when my Dad was so overwhelmed with the heavy task of choosing Kayla's gravestone that he had to pull over his car, sobbing and begging God to touch him with Kayla's presence—and seconds later, our local Christian radio station played "Butterfly Kisses," a song of special significance between Dad and Kayla since she was a little girl. And the time Amber brought flowers to the cemetery and sat by Kayla's graveside, crying, and looked up to see an adult deer standing still and staring her in the eyes from ten feet away. Amber called my Mom, who hurried to meet her there, and then slowly approached the deer to pet it. *That* wasn't happening. The deer bolted, and Amber and Mom chased the poor animal around the fenced cemetery, videotaping the whole ordeal, until the Nebraska Humane Society arrived to catch and release it. Kayla's cemetery is in the middle of the city. The cemetery's ground-crew manager told Mom he's only seen one other deer on the property in 15 years—and no one chased it around with a video camera.

I also found comfort in dreams. I do not know whether God inspired them or whether they were the products of my own subconscious coping efforts, but I do know they brought me immense peace. In some, Kayla and I just chatted, and I was completely unaware of her accident. In others, I was hyperaware that Kayla was in heaven, that I was on earth, and that our time together would end with my dream. In these, I usually just held Kayla and kissed her head, bawling profusely and thanking God for letting her visit me. In one vivid vision, I became aware of Kayla's passing mid-dream. In that dream, Kayla called me on the phone, and we spoke for a minute or two. But then it occurred to me: *Wait—you died. How are we talking?* To which Kayla laughed and replied: *Haven't you ever heard of angels?!* I got quiet, and I thought to myself: *This isn't real.* As soon as disbelief crossed my mind, I realized Kayla wasn't on the line anymore. And then it hit me: *Kayla was with me until I started doubting.* Anxiously, I exclaimed: *Kayla, come back, I believe! I want to keep talking!* Without hesitation, Kayla joyfully chimed back: *I'm still here!!*

Kayla's life and death changed the trajectory of the Youth for Christ in our community, and the spiritual lives of its attendees. The week after the crash was Youth for Christ's last meeting of the year. The group's attendance tripled that night, and five students prayed to receive Jesus Christ as their personal savior, telling the high school group leader, Jason, that they knew "there was something special about Kayla," and they "want[ed] what Kayla had." Jason and his wife, Christy, were at a career crossroads when the accident struck, he later told me. They were soon expecting their first child and had no family in Nebraska. Besides, they had always assumed Omaha was a short-term stop in their young youth-ministry careers. But when Kayla and Nick died, leaving so much hurt among the students they served, they knew their work in Omaha was unfinished. Now, almost ten years later, Jason is the Executive Director of the Omaha-area Youth for Christ. The group has doubled in size during his tenure, now ministering to twice as many students in twice as many schools. In Jason's words, "Christy and I look back at the accident as being the most significant event in why we are still in Omaha. God used (and continues to use!) it in our lives!"

And Kayla lives on—quite literally—in the lives of at least 22 individuals whose lives have been restored from her body tissues. Kayla's cornea brought back one woman's vision; her ligaments helped a 13 year-old boy recover from a devastating knee injury; her bones have been used in numerous spinal-fusion surgeries for men and women in their 50s. All told, Kayla's donations have helped heal people as far west as Colorado and as far east as Maryland, New Jersey, and North Carolina, covering almost every Midwestern state in between.

"God 1st. Others 2nd. Me last." Kayla wouldn't have had it any other way.

*   *   *

In a few parts of this book, I will step outside of the story for some personal reflections. Just a brief pause to chew on and share some things I think I've learned on my journey, and which I hope might help you on yours.

Here, some thoughts on prayer seem appropriate. How does prayer work? What should we pray for? What is the point?

For most of my life, prayer has befuddled me. Jesus' words in the New Testament seem pretty clear when he says, "You may ask me for anything in my name, and I will do it." (John 14:14) Or, "I tell you the truth, if you have faith as small as a mustard seed, you can say to this mountain, 'Move from here to there' and it will move. Nothing will be impossible for you." (Matthew 17:20) But my experience does not harmonize with Jesus' words. In my reality, sometimes—perhaps more often than not—the things I pray for most diligently seldom pan out the way I ask. Looking back from childhood on, I see that this disappointment pops up not only in my more selfish prayers (winning a little-league baseball

36

game; marrying my seventh-grade crush; acing an accounting exam), but also for prayers which seem intrinsically, objectively, uncontroversially good—wishing away a loved one's cancer; asking God to spare the life of a friend's newborn baby; or praying for rain in a famished, drought-stricken land. For me, Kayla's death epitomized a lifetime of fears and inklings that God didn't listen to, or care about, my prayers. I had never wanted anything more or begged God more sincerely, yet my little sister left me in a heartbeat. It seemed there were only two logical conclusions: either Jesus' promises were hollow, or my faith was smaller than a mustard seed. Either way, I saw little reason for optimism.

Pastor George Moore—a man I respect dearly and will introduce later in this book—spent his entire career in ministry and concluded, in some of the simplest and most honest words I've heard on the topic: "I have to tell you: I don't know how prayer works." Pastor George summed up his best understanding of prayer as follows: "We pray; we see miracles; and we struggle." The struggles are constant components of prayer—and they always have been. They just don't always get the same air time as the Bible's great victories. For instance, the most popular psalm in the Bible bravely boasts that with God on our side, "Even though I walk through the darkest valley, I will fear no evil, for you are with me . . . " (Psalm 23) But how often do we reflect on chapter 88 of the same book, where the psalmist desperately searches for God's presence in vain, asking: "Why, O Lord, do you reject me and hide your face from me? . . . The darkness is my closest friend." (Psalm 88) Throughout the psalms, expressions of victory go hand-in-hand with feelings of profound disappointment.

Even the Son of God experienced gut-wrenching disappointment in prayer. On the night before he was crucified, as the mob bore down on him, Jesus prayed in anguish, sweating blood: "Father, if you are willing, take this cup from me; yet not my will, but yours be done." (Luke 22:42) God did not take Jesus' cup from him. He let Jesus suffer, prompting Jesus to cry out from the cross hours later: "My God, my God, why have you forsaken me?" (Matthew 27:26; Mark 15:34) Jesus begged for relief. But God's grand vision required Jesus' temporary suffering and disappointment. The miracle God was performing went beyond even Jesus; it went *through* Jesus *to all of the world.* Big disappointment; *eternal* victory.

So what does this tell us about prayer, and about how we should pray? The Bible seems to contemplate a constant prayerful dialogue with God and expressly empowers us to bring our heart's desires to his feet: "Do not be anxious about anything, but in everything, by prayer and petition, with thanksgiving, present your requests to God." (Philippians 4:6) But the next verse reminds us that the peace God brings in response to our prayers "transcends all understanding." This passage implies that God's understanding runs at a different, higher level than our own incomplete perceptions of a situation. Although there's nothing wrong with praying for a particular outcome, we must recognize that when we do, our prayer limits God's response to (a) fulfilling our specific request, or (b) denying it. God's vision is bigger than the multiple-choice exams we draw up for him. By his very nature, God is "able to do immeasurably more *than all we ask or imagine.*" (Ephesians 3:20) So difficult as it may be, God asks us to trust in his promise for our lives: "'For I know the plans I have for you,' declares the Lord, 'plans to prosper you and not to harm you, plans to give you hope and a future.'" (Jeremiah 29:11) And while God wants us to express our heart's desires to him, we should also seek—and be prepared to accept—his good and perfect will.

Unanswered prayers may be hardest to accept in the context of suffering. We cannot know why we experience hardships now. Maybe God permits the pain in hopes that it will draw us closer to him. Or to help us learn a lesson that we'll someday use to teach someone else. Maybe a much grander design is at play. Perhaps we hold only a single piece of an intricate jigsaw puzzle, while God holds the cover of the box. Maybe pain, despair, and disappointment naturally flow from the free will God gave us, and he cannot cleanly mend every wound without upsetting the choice-driven balance he intended. Whatever the answer may be, Romans 8 tells us we can take solace in the promise that "in all things God works for the good of those who love him," and "our present sufferings are not worth comparing with the glory that will be revealed in us." When our world crashes down around us, God's enduring love for us will stand strong. And in the end, that is all we really need: "Whoever comes to me will never be hungry, and whoever believes in me will never be thirsty." (John 6:35)

In some ways, this may feel unsatisfying. Like the creator of a rigged carnival game, it seems God cannot lose: we thank him for the miracles and trust him through the despair. "Friends, if prayer is anything, it is an act of faith," Pastor George said. I believe I've seen God work miracles—the calls from Kayla's cell phone, the restoration of health where science had ruled it out, and other events I will share later. I've also prayed my heart out and heard crickets. But in an act of faith, I still choose to believe in God—through highs and lows, great victories and profound disappointments. God sent his Son to die for me. What more could he do to gain my trust? When we recognize that the psalmists and Jesus himself sometimes experienced bitter distance from God and the despair that comes from unanswered prayers, it may become more bearable for us to trudge through our own spiritual valleys. Appreciating the struggles that define prayer may not lessen the blow when painful life events strike, but it gives us hope that sunnier days await if we faithfully weather the storm. *An act of faith*—the hallmark of prayer.

CHAPTER 4

"The soul is elastic, like a balloon. It can grow larger through suffering. Loss can enlarge its capacity for anger, depression, despair, and anguish, all natural and legitimate emotions whenever we experience loss. Once enlarged, the soul is also capable of experiencing greater joy, strength, peace, and love. What we consider opposites—east and west, night and light, sorrow and joy, weakness and strength, anger and love, despair and hope, death and life—are no more mutually exclusive than winter and sunlight. The soul has the capacity to experience these opposites, even at the same time."
—JERRY SITTSER, *A GRACE DISGUISED*

In the weeks following Kayla's accident, my parents suffered the worst-possible version of empty-nest syndrome. In what seemed like an instant, they felt stripped of two children—their youngest, who died, and their oldest, who married and moved hundreds of miles away. Only Amber remained in Omaha, and she would soon move into her own apartment. My parents' vacuous five-bedroom home stood as a monument to their newfound loneliness, the deafening silence an ever-present reminder that their family had changed forever. For years, Kayla's room sat virtually untouched: her bed perfectly made, her cheerleading uniform ironed and hanging in the closet, her walls covered with increasingly dated posters and pop-culture references.

The baby of the family, I suspect, always holds a special place in her parents' hearts. But, as I later discovered, a set of unique and very sensitive circumstances magnified my parents' appreciation for Kayla's birth, and their grief over her death.

My parents married on May 24, 1980. Dad had just turned 22, and Mom was a few weeks shy of 20. Their wedding was love-filled but modest: Mom and Aunt Kelly sang at the ceremony, and my maternal grandparents hosted a short reception in the church basement, offering guests cake, mints, and soda. (Dad's side of the family wondered openly, "Where is the beer?!")

From the get-go, money was tight. Dad earned a promotion at work that summer, bumping his annual salary to about $12,000. This, combined with Mom's job teaching preschool, helped my parents eek out a down payment for their first home—a two-bedroom, 1,260 square-foot condo just off the interstate. My parents shared one car, creating logistical challenges as Dad took night classes to complete his bachelor's degree at the University of Nebraska-Omaha.

A little more than a month after the wedding, Mom experienced some medical irregularities, so she saw her doctor. A subdued panic swept over her when she learned the results of her routine urine test: she was pregnant. *No, no, no—that's not possible*, Mom thought. Until that moment, the potential for pregnancy was not even on her radar. She had dutifully taken her birth control during the past ten weeks; indeed, she had taken the pill precisely because my parents knew they were not prepared—financially or emotionally—to have a baby so early in their marriage. With Mom still reeling, the doctor delivered more hard news: because Mom took birth-control medication during the first month of her pregnancy, the baby was at higher risk for birth defects—a commonly held belief at the time.

"Shocked, scared, and numb" are the words Mom used to describe her feelings about these events thirty-two years later, when she shared them with me for the first time. As Mom walked out of the clinic on that summer morning in 1980, the most basic thought pervading her mind was *I cannot be a mother*. At the time she felt, in some ways, like she was still a child herself. The notion of carrying, delivering, and raising her own was surreal and terrifying. She shared the news and her gut reaction with

Dad when he got home from class that night. From there, their mutual fears and the uncertainties seemed to stack and snowball. How could they afford a child? Babies are expensive; they would need a second car; Mom would have to quit her job; and already, they were barely getting by each month. Dad had three years of night school left. Would he be able to keep taking classes while working full-time? The seemingly high likelihood that their baby might be a special-needs child only compounded my parents' financial concerns and Mom's unshakeable feeling that she was ill-equipped for what lay ahead. Today, my parents recall these worries as "stupid rationalizations," but at the time, the daunting realities seemed to point them inescapably toward one solution: abortion.

*   *   *

We sometimes have a stunning ability to rationalize our own bad behaviors. At moral crossroads, we can become willfully blind, stifling our hearts' whispers about what is right so we can do what we know is wrong. Our misdeeds may be recurring, or they can happen in an instant. But in different forms and degrees, sin affects all of us. Even the Apostle Paul—the Christian church's most prominent early missionary and author of nearly half the books of the New Testament—described himself as "unspiritual, sold as a slave to sin," explaining: "I do not understand what I do. For what I want to do, I do not do; but what I hate, I do." (Romans 7:14-15)

Although I've tried in the preceding paragraphs to give a glimpse into my parents' shared mindset a few months into their young marriage, none of this aims to justify or explain their decision. In truth, Mom and Dad *knew*—then and now—that human life, *their baby's life*, had intrinsic value that couldn't be weighed in dollars and cents or in units of convenience, and that a child's special-needs status does not subtract from its dearness. My parents were Christians and lifelong churchgoers. They loved the Lord. They taught Sunday School, and Mom sang solos during worship service. Yet they suspended their moral codes, rationalizing their way to a conclusion with which their spirits could not harmonize.

Probably the truest, most basic explanation for my parents' decision is that decent people can make life-changing mistakes. As Jesus said: "The spirit is willing. But the flesh is so weak." (Matthew 26:41)

* * *

On a warm Friday morning, July 1980—one week after Mom learned she was pregnant—my parents drove to the local clinic and sat in a stuffed waiting room with dozens of other young anxious couples facing—or running away from—unplanned pregnancies. Dad borrowed $300 for the procedure, half of its cost, from a close friend. They told almost no one, partly out of shame and partly because, Mom later said, she was afraid she could be talked out of it. After a brief private consultation, the nurse escorted Mom into the operating room where a doctor performed the procedure, short-circuiting my parents' would-be firstborn's life with stunning swiftness as its soul passed to eternity before its lungs could take their first breath. The entire visit took less than an hour.

Mom remembers almost none of this; before, during, and after the procedure, she put up a sort of mental block that allowed her to move on without ever directly dealing with her emotions. Dad, on the other hand, was unable to set aside his feelings or the tugging gravity of what they had done. His regret was heavy and immediate. After the procedure, he drove Mom to a pharmacy for antibiotics, waited for her to go inside, and then sunk his head onto the steering wheel, bawling profusely. My parents' emotional dichotomy played out like this for decades: Dad wanting to sort through and discuss their shared painful experience, and bringing it up once every year or two—using mutually understood references like "what happened" or simply "1980" because the word "abortion" was too awful to say—and Mom flatly replying "I don't want to talk about it," or just leaving the room, until Dad eventually stopped trying. As Mom explained later, "If we talked about it, it would be true."

And so "1980" remained my parents' unspeakable secret, their festering guilt building within them and spilling over in ways not easy to trace. Years later, our church's congregation began to gather once a month outside the abortion clinic—the same one my parents visited for their procedure—in silent prayer for changed hearts and saved lives. Dad could not go; it all felt too hypocritical. He had determined he would tell me, Amber, and Kayla the truth, together, when we were all adults. Until then, he waited, his fear of worldly condemnation hanging over his head ceaselessly. Even a decade after the fact, my parents could count on one hand the number of people who knew about their terminated pregnancy. One of them was a pastor who Dad confided in and tried to emphasize to Dad the infinite depth of God's grace and mercy. "I knew God had forgiven me," Dad later said, "but I could not forgive myself." The pastor asked Dad if he could share my parents' experience, on an anonymous basis, with other young couples he counseled who were also considering abortion. Dad agreed. Two years later, the pastor called Dad and told him that at least eight couples had decided to follow through with their pregnancies based, in part, on my parents' story. The news came as a mixed blessing: Dad was relieved to hear some good had finally come from this, but wondered how many more lives he was failing to reach by continuing to hide behind his shame.

After Amber was born, Mom was diagnosed with a prolapsed uterus. The trauma of two deliveries had weakened and damaged her abdominal cavity's lining and ligaments so badly, her doctors said, that she could no longer have kids. This was not an option for Mom, though. She and Dad had always wanted three children. She felt she had voluntarily "given away one baby" and considered it the worst mistake of her life. She could not undo the past, but she would try everything in her power to have a third child. So in December 1986, Mom elected to undergo uterine suspension surgery—an invasive, time-consuming procedure in which ligaments were removed from her back and reattached in her abdomen to support her uterus. Even with the surgery, my parents understood their chances for a successful third pregnancy were not the best. But just before Christmas the next year, during Mom's one-year post-operative follow-up, she was delighted with the same news that had so terrified her seven years before: she was pregnant. From then on, my parents considered Kayla their "miracle baby," a living reminder and perfect embodiment of God's forgiveness for the sins of their past.

*   *   *

For my parents, the line connecting July 1980 to Kayla's accident almost 24 years later was clear and direct. In fact, this link is the last thing Mom remembers making before she passed out in the emergency room after Kayla's doctor told her he didn't think Kayla would survive. As Mom put it, "God took Kayla away because I took my child's life away ... it was my fault." Mom didn't wonder whether she was being punished by God; she *knew* she was being punished by God, she said. Her self-accusations persisted for years. She endured them alone, and silently. In a way, she felt responsible for taking the lives of two of her children—one by choice, and the other as divine retribution for her sins.

In the months and years following Kayla's death, we saw a troubling, gradual shift in Mom's demeanor. She seemed perpetually groggy, as if she were always falling into or emerging from sleep. At times, she slurred words or tuned out of conversations, leaning back in her chair or even closing her eyes unless she was directly engaged. She missed lunch appointments with friends and other commitments with Dad, sometimes without notice or explanation. With every passing month, she seemed to be transforming from her former social, cheery self into someone we didn't completely recognize.

For Dad, this period marked the first time when he wondered whether, and how, their marriage would survive. My parents had received ample warning: among the hundreds of sympathy cards that flooded their home following Kayla's death, nearly twenty came from fellow mothers and fathers who had lost children and who cautioned my parents that their relationship would be rigorously tested in the wake of their tragedy. At first, Dad dismissed this counsel; he and Mom would always stand together, in good times and bad, just as they promised each other on their wedding day. But uncertainty crept in on the 88th day after Kayla's passing. This was the first day that Dad did not weep for his lost daughter. This was the first morning in which Dad woke up feeling, for the most part, happy and hopeful for the day ahead. But Mom was in a different place. She woke up in deep despair, pulling Dad down with her. The next day, their positions flipped: Mom was ready for a decent day, and Dad grieved heavily. Dad began to wonder whether they would ever again be happy *together*; whether they could simultaneously enjoy each other's company.

As Mom's disposition worsened in the years following Kayla's death, Dad worried that she might be "slipping away" for good—that she had irreversibly succumbed to the burden of a decades-long cycle of shame, internalization, and grief. He had no other explanation for why Mom was changing. From time to time, he thought *I don't know how much longer I can deal with this*. Dad's guilt weighed heavily upon him, too—not just for the abortion itself, but because he felt he had failed his wife and bore responsibility for her decline. Mom had always welcomed Dad's role as leader in their relationship, but at the most pivotal moment of their young marriage—1980, when Mom was frightened and utterly lost—he had done nothing to dissuade her from making a decision he knew would haunt them forever.

During this time, Dad clung to the Bible and to his prayer routine like never before. One morning in early 2008—about 3 ½ years after Kayla's accident, and at the pinnacle of our family's concerns about Mom—Dad sat at the desk in his home office, praying for his marriage and for God's guidance and patience. Suddenly, without any reason or identifiable prompting, Dad spun around in his swivel chair and gazed toward the opposite corner of the office, where he saw three shoeboxes tucked discretely underneath a shelving unit. Dad had passed by these boxes hundreds of times before without paying any attention to them. But on this occasion, almost unconsciously, Dad walked toward the boxes, set the top two aside, and went straight for the bottom box. When he opened it, he found nearly two-dozen bottles of stashed medications prescribed to Mom—Xanax, Seroquel, and a potluck of other pills used to treat various disorders, but never in such potent and redundant combinations. "It was absolutely a God thing," Dad later said. "I was not looking for anything. Something just told me to go to the corner and open that box."

When confronted with the shoebox, Mom did not deny that she had collected the prescriptions and had come to depend on them as an antidote to her despair. She also did not deny that she had hidden the pills from Dad. Over time, the medicines had given her severe stomach aches and recurring ulcers, but they also helped her to temporarily forget her loss and guilt. "I didn't think I was strong enough to deal with the pain by myself," she said. "The medicine helped me to get through the day without thinking about it." That day, Mom stopped taking the vast majority of her prescribed medications, cold turkey. Her disposition improved almost immediately. The hard days still came and went, like waves, some ebbing and some crashing. But once she faced the pain instead of cloaking it, she could more fully rely on *God's* power—in whatever form it might take each day—to carry her through them. She didn't have to run away or face the pain alone. And she finally had hope that, in time, the joyful days would outnumber the sad.

*   *   *

Shame and regret are heavy loads to carry. For some, my parents' story might hit close to home—particularly the way our gravest mistakes can alter our self-perceptions and weigh on our spiritual lives. Certainly, when it comes to avoiding the things we should do while doing the things we should avoid, I suspect most of us can identify. For *"all have sinned and fall short of the glory of God."* (Romans 3:23)

But sin, shame, and regret don't get the last word. Because the very next verse promises us that despite our mistakes, *"all are justified freely* by his grace through the redemption that came by Christ Jesus." (Romans 3:24) Indeed, "God so loved the world that he gave his one and only Son, that whoever believes in him shall not perish but have eternal life." (John 3:16) The take-home point is that God's grace is your sin's mirror opposite—only infinitely stronger and purer, enabling it to counteract, overpower, and wipe clean the dirt you see on yourself. And *absolutely nothing*—not your biggest regret, not your most shameful addiction, not the mistakes you have made, or are making, or will make— can remove you from grace's healing reach. "For I am convinced," Paul wrote, "that neither death nor life, neither angels nor demons, neither the present nor the future, nor any powers, neither height nor depth, nor anything else in all creation, will be able to separate us from the love of God that is in Christ Jesus our Lord." (Romans 8:38-39)

The trouble with grace is that it doesn't make a lick of sense. It contradicts more familiar virtues, like justice. The nearly 4,000-year-old Code of Hammurabi metes out ancient instructions for redressing wrongs: "An eye for an eye, a tooth for a tooth." The Old Testament painstakingly reinforces the same principle of reciprocity: "Life for life . . . hand for hand, foot for foot, burn for burn, wound for wound . . . " (Exodus 21:23-25) Today, our aptly named "justice system" incorporates modern concepts of retribution to punish and deter crimes. Through tradition and necessity, notions of fairness and justice permeate all facets of our lives—our perceptions and reactions, our relationships, our laws and government, our jobs, and even how we see ourselves.

Because of these deeply ingrained values, it is sometimes hard for us to forgive ourselves and move forward from our past mistakes and corresponding regret. We feel spiritually out of sync, stuck in the stink of our shame and weighed down by moral debts we cannot repay. *If I can barely stand myself,* we may ask, *how could God ever accept me?* But the pardoning of sins isn't your jurisdiction. It's God's, and *he has chosen to forgive you*—unconditionally and always. Jesus' life and death shattered tradition, tipping justice's scales forever in our favor. For "while we were still sinners, Christ died for us," substituting his life for ours and willfully accepting the ultimate punishment in love's exchange for our sins. (Romans 5:8) Jesus' sacrifice was necessary to atone for us because "the wages of sin is death." (Romans 6:23) But Jesus' blood forged a "new covenant . . . poured out for many for the forgiveness of sins." (Matthew 26:28) As a result, "there is now no condemnation for those who are in Christ Jesus, because through Christ Jesus the law of the Spirit who gives life has set you free from the law of sin and death." (Romans 8:1-2) In other words, God so loves you and me that he sent his own Son to bridge the divide separating God's perfect nature from our sin-stained selves. And now, our bond to God's love is so strong that nothing can break it.

Although we cannot know the mind of God, I don't think Christ paid our debts to recoup on them later, with deferred interest. I don't think God forgave my Mom and collected on Kayla, as Mom feared for so long. This represents the kind of old-school thinking that Jesus upended. When his disciples saw a blind man on the side of a road, they asked, "Rabbi, who sinned, this man or his parents, that he was born blind?" "Neither," Jesus said, as he restored the man's sight: "This happened so that the works of God might be displayed in him." It wasn't about the sin. It was about Christ's goodness. And lucky for you and me, Jesus never shied away from fix-up projects. The same Savior who invested in lepers, prostitutes, and tax collectors aches to work a miracle in us, too. "For God did not send his Son into the world to condemn the world, but to *save the world through him*." (John 3:17)

Like any great gift, the point of grace isn't to make sense of it or to justify it. The point is to accept it with open hands and deepest thanks. God knows we are like "jars of clay"—earthly, chipped, cracked, and broken. But he pours his grace into us anyhow. For it's through our imperfections that God's light shines best, "to show that this all-surpassing power is from God and not from us." (2 Corinthians 4:7) So let God's light shine through your brokenness. Let his grace pour into and over you, wiping clean your mirror to reveal the pure, radiant image God sees in you. The gift's been given—you just need to receive it.

CHAPTER 5

"Do not conform any longer to the pattern of this world, but be transformed by the renewing of your mind. Then you will be able to test and approve what God's will is—his good, pleasing, and perfect will."
—ROMANS 12:2

Imagine, if you can, the Incas' bewilderment when Pizarro and his band of pasty, bearded, uniformed men first anchored their ships off of the Peruvian coast. Or the disorientation a family dog feels when its masters leave for the hospital and come home with a tiny, fussy, stinky newborn. Well, *I* don't have to wonder. Because I experienced the same kind of lost-in-translation confusion with Amber, the older of my two younger sisters, at all times throughout our childhood. *What is this thing you call "girl?"* I wondered, the first time I met Baby Amber. *Why does it cry so much? And what happens if you cross your eyes at it? Or flick it?*

As time passed, Amber grew ever more perplexing. How could she show so little interest in my impressive baseball-card collection? Or forts?! How could she chat idly on the phone *during a Huskers game?!* I knew instinctively that farts were funny. So why did Amber act so offended when I hopped on her lap and let one rip? Perhaps most mind-boggling was Amber's categorical rejection of all games and sports. One year, my parents signed Amber up for a YMCA softball league. Dad bought Amber a glove, and the pair trotted to the backyard to practice. But when Dad tossed a glorious pop fly into the summer sky, Amber stuck up her glove, closed her eyes, and totally whiffed; the ball plunked her right between the eyes. And that was the end of Amber's softball career.

Amber became my unlikely ally in one shared passion, though: playing pranks on our maternal grandmother. We loved to scheme. We put pine needles in grandma's slippers; we hid her TV remote in hilarious places, like the freezer; we chewed up gum and used it to plaster grandma's dental floss to her bathroom drawer.   Nothing was off limits.   But we weren't laughing when Christmas came around, and grandma gave me a stocking full of coal (and nothing else).   Or the next week, when grandma decorated Amber's birthday cake with trick relighting candles.   Amber *loved* frosting, so the instant she blew out her candles, she plucked one out of the cake and licked its waxy end.   Unfortunately for her, the wick reignited mid-lick, scorching the tip of Amber's nose.   For the next couple of days, Amber looked like Snoopy.   After that incident, we called a truce with grandma.

Amber and I even *looked* like opposites.   For most of my childhood, I was on the scrawny side, with fair skin, a slight lisp, and boxy, brown-framed glasses that covered half of my face.   I joke now (but cried then) that I was an ubergeek, assembled from the parts of lesser geeks.   Amber, on the other hand, was attractive and cool.   (To confirm this, all you had to do was ask her.)   She had dark features, olive skin, and wavy sandy-blond hair.   It was as if my parents had saved up their "pretty genes" for Amber so as not to expend them on me.   Amber's looks came with a downside, though, as she dealt with pressures—both self-imposed and external—that I never faced.   Dad sometimes tells people, only half-kiddingly, that two of his three kids (me and Kayla) were on "autopilot" during childhood—that is, we were the easy kids, practically raising ourselves.   Amber required much more active navigation—she had a herky-jerky manual transmission, erratic brakes, and no power steering.

Early on, it seemed like a battle was brewing for Amber's soul.   At times, she could be alarmingly materialistic, wrapping up her identity in her clothes, her popularity, and her attention from boys.   But other times, she could be sweet and introspective.   After a church mission trip to an impoverished Mexican town in eighth grade, Amber was struck by how content the Mexican children were with so little, while Amber acknowledged that she was unhappy with so much.   Upon returning from the trip, Amber threw away her rap CDs, gave away loads of clothes, and refocused on her walk with God.   But Amber's self-worth struggles continued.

Some studies estimate that 7 million American women suffer from an eating disorder. Amber was one of them. Anorexia and bulimia may be triggered and perpetuated by numerous influences—social, cultural, genetic, hormonal—and may touch upon core aspects of the victim's emotional well-being like self-image, control, fear, and coping. Because I have never personally experienced an eating disorder, my insight here is necessarily limited, observational, and secondhand. Nonetheless, I tread into the topic to provide an honest and accurate portrayal of this part of the story.

My suspicions arose when Amber was thirteen years old. My Mom bought a ten-pack of Reese's peanut butter cups on a Saturday night, and when I woke up on Sunday morning, they were gone . . . *all* of them. No one in my family admitted to eating any, even though I found the wrappers buried in the bottom of the kitchen trash can. As instances like this stacked up, it became a sort of family joke: our house, we said, was haunted by a very peculiar ghost. One that had no interest in terrorizing us, but just wanted to devour our Little Debbie's. But over time, we suspected something more ominous was at play.

During Amber's sophomore year of high school, she and my Dad took a weekend father-daughter trip to Chicago. As was customary for Amber, she ate little during the day. She did, however, blow the bulk of her souvenir allowance on two bags of assorted candy. In the middle of the night, Amber got up from her hotel-room bed, and Dad listened as she inhaled the first full bag in a frenzy, and then turned to the second bag, which she also put a major dent in. Then Amber slipped away to the bathroom, where she ran a faucet to disguise the noise and remained for several minutes before returning to bed. Throughout high school, this was Amber's modus operandi: to nearly starve herself during the day, and to binge and purge herself in the dead of the night. It was very difficult to catch her in the act, and even when we did, Amber brushed off our concerns, insisting that she was just hungry for a midnight snack, or not feeling well, and that we were the strange ones for suggesting otherwise.

Years later, when Kayla passed away, my parents grieved together. I leaned heavily on Beth. But Amber endured it alone.

Amber attempted to counter her grief and loneliness with a series of empty and ultimately disappointing relationships. There was Bachelor #1, who cheated on Amber and left her. Then there was the much-older Bachelor #2, with his estranged children and his multiple drunk-driving citations, who, judicially stripped of his driver's license, required Amber to chauffeur him everywhere. It seemed there was never a pause between Amber's relationships; as soon as one came to an upsetting end, the next one began.

And so things began with Brad in late 2005. Like almost every other guy Amber dated, Brad was, according to Amber, "the one." He had a good family and a steady job, and he treated Amber, she often said, "like a princess." Much of this was verifiably true: Brad's parents and brothers *were* kind people; Brad *did* demonstrate a strong work ethic, waking up before 5 a.m. to load a truck and deliver furniture for a local retailer six days a week; and Brad *did* pamper Amber with gifts—the new iPhone, designer purses, and anything else for which Amber was all too willing to bat her eyelashes and ask. At first blush, Brad looked menacing: towering and muscular, with tattoos and pit bulls. But Brad was also polite and soft-spoken; he was artistically gifted, once drawing my parents a beautiful portrait of Kayla; and he showed sincere interest in being a part of our family, regularly joining my parents for dinner and attending our family holiday gatherings.

My parents bit their tongue and gritted their teeth when Amber announced she was moving in with Brad. Just a few months later, Amber made a bigger announcement: she was pregnant. At first, the news was difficult for my conservative parents. But they were also delighted to welcome their first grandchild, and they were proud of Amber's courage in keeping her baby, especially given their own history.

On Easter Sunday, 2007, with Amber less than two months pregnant, Brad slapped Amber for the first time. It happened during a minor argument in Brad's car. Amber was shocked; she cowered into the corner of her passenger-side seat and whimpered until they got home. And she told no one, neither then nor in the months that followed, as the frequency and magnitude of Brad's aggression escalated unchecked.

Amber gave birth to a baby boy, Bailey, on November 30, 2007. One year later, Brad and Amber were engaged. Through selective avoidance of her friends and family, myriad excuses, and heavy doses of makeup, Amber hid the intensifying hostility of her domestic reality. She saw a doctor who prescribed her anti-anxiety medication to quell her growing panic attacks. Out of equal parts fear and love, Amber stayed with Brad and did not report the abuse: fear because Amber had learned to be submissive to Brad, not defiant of him, and she did not know whether she could raise Bailey on her own; love because she cared about Brad, both as her partner and as Bailey's father, and she believed he loved her too.

The violence reached a breaking point on Friday night, January 23, 2009. Brad and Amber had a night out, with Brad's mother babysitting Bailey. According to police reports, the two were at a bar, and Amber said something that embarrassed Brad in front of his friends. When they got home, Brad "dragged [Amber] up the stairs by her hair and into their apartment," where he "hit her in the face with an open and closed fist." At six-foot-four and 240 pounds, Brad was literally more than twice Amber's size. When Amber returned to Brad's parents' home later that evening to pick up Bailey, Brad's mother saw Amber's face and immediately called 911.

The police arrived to find Amber "shaken," "hysterical," "afraid," and crying, with a "deep bruise" on her chin, "a bruised left cheek bone," and swelling redness around her right eye. After they called for reinforcements, the police found Brad in the apartment complex's parking lot asleep in his car, engine running, with a loaded handgun in his jacket, a shotgun in his trunk, and a blood-alcohol level nearly twice the legal limit. Brad was charged with third-degree domestic assault, carrying a concealed weapon, and driving under the influence. He pled guilty and served a 105-day sentence.

I wish I could say that this episode ended a sad chapter of Amber's life, but I cannot. In reality, Amber welcomed Brad back the day he was released from jail for abusing her. But finally, six months later, Amber was ready to break free from the cycle of violence. She hired an attorney to secure a protection order against Brad and to establish her sole legal custody of Bailey. Amber also earned her cosmetology certificate and landed a job selling beauty products for Peel's Salon Services. Her confidence soared. She called me to pass along each compliment she received from work supervisors; she took up jogging, hauling Bailey around Lake Zorinsky in an all-terrain stroller; and she and Bailey started attending Lifegate Church together, just the two of them. By Fall 2010, for the first time in a long time in Amber's life, things were looking up.

Amber's difficulties branched into many different forms, but all were rooted in the same lack of self-value and struggle for identity. *Why do I matter? What defines me? My image? My belongings? My boyfriend? Or something else?*

It's so easy to get wrapped up in the things of this world. On a good day, I spend about 15 minutes in prayer or reading scripture. That's 1% of my time. If you are anything like I am, maybe we shouldn't be surprised when we find ourselves overidentifying with the earthly things that make up the majority of our time and the bulk of our energy—our relationships, our jobs, our possessions, etc. These self-made measuring sticks can only disappoint us. No significant other will make us whole; someone will always be skinnier, or smarter, or wealthier, or more successful, or drive a nicer car. When we die, these things that consumed us for so long—even seizing our identities—will become instantly irrelevant. As the saying goes, you never see a hearse pulling a U-Haul.

We are not our zip codes. We are not our business cards. We are not our bank accounts, or our shoes, or our partner's partner. Above all, when we receive God's great love, we become *"children of God"*: "And that is what we are!" (1 John 3:1) As God's children, we were created for a purpose, "fearfully and wonderfully." (Psalm 139:14) Our worthiness does not need to be (nor can it be) earned. Rather, we are *inherently worthy*, infused with inestimable value, merely because God chose to create us; because we are alive; and because we are his. Indeed, God cared for us "even before [we] were born." (Isaiah 44:2) He knows the number of hairs on our heads. (Luke 12:7) "You know me inside out, you know every bone in my body" proclaims the psalmist. "You know exactly how I was made, bit by bit, how I was sculpted from nothing into something." (Psalm 139:15) Because of our inspired nature, earthly things can never quench our spiritual thirsts. Our true fulfillment only comes from knowing, loving, and serving God—our Creator. "Do not love the world or anything in the world," the Bible tells us. For "the world and its desires pass away, but whoever does the will of God lasts forever." (1 John 2:15-17)

Like so many spiritual things, embracing our roles as God's children while facing life's day-to-day reality is easier in theory than in practice. But if we allow it, God's love can transform us. "Therefore, if anyone is in Christ, he is a *new creation*; the old has gone, the new has come!" (2 Corinthians 5:17) In some ways, the task of connecting to our spiritual identities may not be altogether different from learning how to play the piano or mastering a new language. There is no "trick"—just a lot of practice and commitment. Ultimately, God seeks to replace our empty ambitions with his lavish love for us—a love that is wider, longer, higher, and deeper than anything we can imagine, filling us "to the measure of all the fullness of God." (Ephesians 3:14-19) By delighting in this love, we receive the deepest desires of our hearts. (Psalm 37:4) Ours is an identity that's pure and everlasting. It's an identity that transforms us and satisfies our souls' longings in a way worldly ambitions cannot. Best of all, tapping into it only requires us to be precisely who God made us to be: his beloved children.

CHAPTER 6

"He must become greater; I must become less."
—JOHN 3:30

Three days after Kayla died, I graduated from college. Some graduates used masking tape to inscribe cute quips on their graduation caps, like "Finally!" or "Got job?" or "I is SMAЯT!" Mine said "Hi Kayla!" I imagined my sister reading it from the heavens and smiling down on me. As I accepted my diploma, I could not stop the tears that seemed to spring from my ducts against my will. The dean of my college hugged me.

My wedding was three weeks later. Beth and I found there was no textbook way to celebrate the biggest, most joyful day of our lives in the wake of our worst tragedy. We felt a difficult tension. The more we paid tribute to Kayla during the ceremony, the more it would feel like a second funeral, not our wedding celebration. But the less we acknowledged Kayla, the more it felt like we were deliberately avoiding her, and the reality of how everyone felt. When one of my groomsmen walked down the aisle with a solitary lit candle in his hand instead of Kayla on his arm, I lost it. From then until "I do," I could not dwell on my love for Beth or the momentousness of our lifelong commitments to each other. Instead, my focus was mostly on *getting through this*. I felt so badly for Beth. There was little we could do about it, but this was not how she dreamt it would be.

Later that summer, we moved to St. Louis, and I started teaching at an inner-city charter school. It took me awhile to realize that when students yelled, "Mr. Wilkins!" they were talking to me. Teaching, I often tell people, was both the best and worst job I ever had. For me, it was governed by the rule of thirds: One in three days, I was the commander of my classroom and felt truly inspired, like I was changing the world, one lesson at a time. One in three days, I was half-teacher and half-babysitter, accomplishing disappointingly little, but hey, it could have gone worse. And one in three days, whatever the trigger—whether it was breaking up another hallway fight, or searching for the proper response when a frustrated student lashed out at me yelling, confusingly, "You shut your mouth when you're talking to me!"—I trudged home, plopped onto the couch, and contemplated quitting.

My time as a teacher was short-lived but chock-full of memorable moments. Like when Jalesa, a seventh-grader, pointed out to her class that everyone she knew was a Democrat, to which Nadia protested "Not me, I'm a Republican!" Jalesa looked Nadia up and down, zeroed in on Nadia's shabby, tattered sneakers (which Nadia's big toes poked through), and retorted "Not with those shoes, you're not!" I loved finding fun new ways to engage my students, like my "math raps" series, in which I mashed educational lyrics to popular songs. For example, "Slow Motion," an embarrassingly explicit song by Juvenile, morphed into "Long Division." During quizzes, I heard students singing it under their breath:

UUUUUUUUHHHH! Divide it like that!
Then multiply it back, find the product, and subtract;
Bring down a digit for me!
Do it again for me!
Find the remainder for me!
THAT'S LONG DIVISION FOR ME!

The next year, I enrolled in law school at Washington University in St. Louis—one of the top law schools in the country, and conveniently located just a few miles from our home. The transition from teacher back to pupil was easy for me; I was one of the few students in my entering class who felt I was "de-stressing" by going to law school. I studied diligently, but I also tried not to take myself too seriously. During my first year, I played on seven different intramural sports teams and seldom missed the law school's weekly happy hours at Wash U's aptly named "Anheuser-Busch Hall."

My favorite moment in law school came during my Property Law class. Our teacher, Professor Gunn, was well-liked but seemingly unobservant, prompting me to claim, exaggeratedly, that I could probably cook a burger in class, and he wouldn't notice. My friend Lauren bet me $1 that I couldn't, and *it was on!* One day toward the end of the semester, I lugged into class a small sack of groceries and a George Foreman grill, which I borrowed from a campus fraternity and smuggled into class by wedging it not-so-inconspicuously between my books. During a set of particularly involved hypothetical questions, I reached down, plugged in the grill, and waited for it to heat up. A moment later, I pretended to shuffle through some notes in my bag, but actually slid a raw chicken breast onto the George Foreman. (Lauren and I had previously stipulated that a chicken sandwich qualified as a "burger" per the terms of our agreement.)

I underestimated two things: first, the way the greasy steamy stench of a seldom-cleaned grill can permeate even a very large room; and second, the intense heat generated in the immediate area of an electric grill—in my case, the area beneath my desk and between my legs. As the chicken slowly sizzled and its aroma wafted across the room, my classmates' heads turned in my general direction like fans doing "the wave" at a baseball game. And by the time the chicken was cooked, my jeans were sweat-soaked up past my knees. But remarkably, Professor Gunn *did not notice!* Or perhaps he smelled something funky or heard a faint sizzling sound, but then thought to himself *I really doubt a student is cooking in my class right now.* How wrong he was. The crowning point was when I reached under the desk, assembled my lunch, and resurfaced to eat my hot, fresh, chicken sandwich mid-lecture, one dollar richer.

Lest I give you the wrong impression that my law-school career was no-work-and-all-play, I feel compelled to note some other highlights: winning the school's annual moot-court competition with my friend and teammate, Ben; serving as an Executive Editor for the Washington University Law Review; and graduating *magna cum laude*, in the top

3% of my class. In the summer of 2008, Beth and I moved to Chicago, where I took a job with Kirkland & Ellis LLP, one of the best law firms in the world for commercial litigation, my chosen practice. But really, who needs all of that when you've got a great chicken sandwich story?

*   *   *

In our early years together, Beth and I created our own fun in the ways that cash-strapped couples often do: picnics and outdoor games in the park; movie nights with a homemade dinner; hitting up all of the free summer concerts we could find. We built homes with Habitat for Humanity, and Beth led our church's youth group, enlisting me as her steady helper. Beth kept singing, at recitals and in coffee shops, and her voice was maturing beautifully. On one funny occasion, Beth surprised me during a show by telling the crowd her next song was dedicated to her loving and supportive husband—me. The audience cooed and awwed sweetly, with dozens of eyes landing on my blushing face. Then, Beth burst into "Mister Snow," a silly musical-theater piece describing a "big bewhiskered," "overbearing" seafarer who "can't seem to lose the smell of fish"—but the singer loves him anyway, eventually declaring that "fish is my favorite perfume!" I feigned embarrassment and chuckled along with the crowd—*well played, Beth*. Throughout our marriage, I loved Beth's warm way of showing affection and felt blessed to be its recipient.

But beneath the surface, my years in St. Louis and Chicago were sometimes very difficult, both emotionally and spiritually. It was surreal leaving my family and Nebraska for the first time right after we lost Kayla. Beth and I were in a new city, a new house, and a new marriage, with new jobs and new friends. Beth was my "home base"—the only link tethering my unfamiliar present to my recent past, which, despite the sadness, I did not want to forget. In the medium-term aftermath of Kayla's passing, this became an ever-present dilemma: when and how to remember. For years, Kayla's loss buzzed about in the pockets of my consciousness, always close, only to emerge, poignantly and unexpectedly, with the slightest trigger—a sentimental song, a movie's hospital scene, or the sight of a little girl at the zoo, for example. People often remind grievers that their lost loved ones live on in the form of happy memories. But my warmest memories—the ones that best captured Kayla's sweet nature and our sibling love—sometimes stung the worst because they painfully reinforced what I'd lost and would never experience again.

For the sake of functioning, I often pushed these rushing feelings down and away the moment I sensed them brewing. In order to manage my day, I just couldn't "go there"; I couldn't reflect on my sister. But the act of aversion, too, came with internal repercussions: the guilty concern that I might be "unremembering" Kayla through selective avoidance. During these years, I relied on Beth so much, sobbing to her every time a sad anniversary or life milestone passed, or when I allowed a new memory of Kayla to hit me. Sometimes I didn't want to bring Beth down with me, so I cried alone in my car or in the shower. Beth often encouraged me to seek counseling, but I never did for a number of unconvincing reasons: I didn't need help; it was expensive; I was too busy; etc.

I also struggled with my so-called "relationship with God," a phrase that too often escaped meaning for me. Ever since I was a child, I feared there might be something wrong with me, spiritually. I remember "accepting Christ" dozens of times, but I never felt a change sweep over me the way some people described. When I prayed, I didn't feel like I was "having a conversation" with God; I felt completely alone, and sometimes rather foolish. *Really, what is the point of praying?*, I often wondered. Kayla's death had taught me that my deepest, most impassioned prayers might go unanswered. I found it hard not to be cynical of Jesus' promise in Mark 11:24: "Therefore I tell you, whatever you ask in prayer, believe that you have received it, and it will be yours." Hadn't I "asked" and "believed" that God would save Kayla's life? Amidst the backdrop of my doubt, when I tried to read the Bible, inconsistently and haphazardly, I found the text distant and archaic, not personal or enlightening; its passages seemed to unravel in the crosshairs of my skepticism.

I never purposely turned away from God. My doubts frustrated me, but when push came to shove, I still believed in him, that he loved me, and that he had called me—literally—the night Kayla died, in an act of love and in answer to my prayer. God was more than living up to his end of the bargain. The problem, I knew, was *me*. *I* seldom sought God through prayer, and even when I did, my mind tended to wander off distractedly. *I* failed to regularly study the Bible and read my devotionals, even when I set specific goals to improve in these areas. And *I* recognized my spiritual immaturity, but I lacked the drive and discipline to do anything about it.

Predictably, my perceived spiritual inadequacies affected my self-image and bled into other areas of my life—most notably my relationship with Beth. At the outset, I should note that the sources of our marital strife were numerous and complex; some problems were primarily mine, some were Beth's, and some were uniquely ours. But out of respect for Beth, and because I can't provide an unbiased telling of a two-sided story, I recount only my own faults here. In my personal life, I felt small; in my marriage, I acted small. At times I could be proud, selfish, critical, quick to anger, slow to forgive, and unable to forget, or to move forward with Beth on a clean slate. When I felt hurt, I sometimes withheld love from Beth and gave her cold shoulders that lasted far too long. In my worst moments during our worst arguments, I even invoked the "D" word: Divorce. I didn't mean it; I loved Beth wholeheartedly and would never leave her. The word was unfair and childish, but a potent ante-upper for our verbal tiffs, designed to underscore the gravity of my disappointment with recurring issues in our marriage. More than anything, though, it was just wrong.

To me, the hurtful things Beth and I said to each other were "just words." *Yes, we say things we don't mean during arguments,* I thought. *But what couple doesn't?* The good times—the holidays, the church events, the game nights, vacations, and sitcom marathons—still far outnumbered the bad times, and our love for and commitment to each other would prevail. I always thought we'd have more time to figure things out, even as Beth and I seemed to dig in our heels and double down on the negative conflict-management patterns that crystallized early in our marriage, under the stifling pressure of our grief and stress. But for Beth, the bad days, and the sadness and anxiety that surrounded them, came to define us. Eventually, she began to see me as more her adversary than her protector, more her critic than her supporter. And for reasons I may never understand, Beth concealed from me the true depths of her concerns and discontent—a fundamental "brokenness" in our marital foundation that Beth later told me she had perceived since the first year of our marriage, but which went forever unrepaired because of Beth's silence and my obliviousness to it. Over the years, each time I thought Beth and I had fully bounced back from conflict, Beth's microscope remained trained on the widening hidden chasm she sensed between us. Until, on the evening of October 11, 2010—as I sat on our living-room sofa, eating a Subway sandwich and watching Monday Night Football, blind to what was about to unfold—Beth came home and crushed me: after six-and-a-half years of marriage, she was finished.

*   *   *

Beth left that night and never came back, except to pack her belongings and say goodbye to our dogs. At a friend's prompting, Beth agreed to join me for a few "mediation" sessions, but our clashing goals made the meetings pointless: while Beth came each week intending to sensitively but firmly convey the finality of her decision and mediate the terms of our divorce, I came begging for reconciliation. Beth's mind was made up. She cut off the sessions after our third visit.

Words alone cannot convey the sick, panicked, bottomless despair that engulfed me during the first few weeks following Beth's news. Some snapshots might paint a clearer picture: irrepressible sobs that overwhelmed my ability to breathe and became wheezes, then coughs, and, in some cases, vomiting; desperate calls, texts, and emails to Beth, her family, and our mutual friends, followed by hours' worth of staring at my phone and computer screen, praying for a response and wondering if I should try again in the meantime; waking up in the middle of the night to the sound of my own groaning. One of my closest friends, Scott—who lived with me in FarmHouse during college and just a few blocks away from me years later in Chicago—prayed and read the Bible with me almost every night. We prayed for a miracle, for a second chance, and honed in on chapters describing how love *should* look, like 1 Corinthians 13, a passage featured in Beth's and my wedding which, tragically, felt like it was just now sinking in for the first time: *"Love is patient, love is kind . . . it is not proud. It does not dishonor others, it is not self-seeking, it is not easily angered, it keeps no record of wrongs . . . It always protects, always trusts, always hopes, always perseveres."* Each description pierced me like a dagger. Love, it seemed—the kind God intended—was everything I wasn't as a husband.

I was stunned by Beth's departure and felt it came without any warning, a fact that, in retrospect, said much about the marital disconnect I had failed to recognize. Aside from shock, I felt so many terrible emotions all at once. One was regret. I had taken Beth for granted, never appreciating that my marriage—like anything else in life—was fragile, and it could break. Like an awful repeating blooper reel, my mind replayed some of our saddest moments: sitting next to Beth in church and stewing over a trivial issue while we listened to a sermon on forgiveness; getting dressed up for a date, only to make a cutting remark that ruined it before it started. I regretted most the times when I had recognized that I was wrong, but my pride prevented me from admitting it and apologizing to Beth because, darn it, she had hurt my feelings too. With each and every wrongful act and omission, I had inched Beth farther away from me. And now, it was too late. *Oh, God, it's too late.* The realization was impossible. *If I could just go back and repeat the past,* I thought, *I would do everything differently!* I would always apologize first, and sincerely. I would love Beth unconditionally, caring for her needs the best that I could, regardless of whether she was trying to meet mine. Because that's how God loved me, and how he taught us to love each other; and because that's what I had promised Beth in my vows to her. I obsessed over every wrong I could recall, punishing myself for not doing and saying the right things while there was still time to act.

I felt totally lost. Every aspect of my life was intertwined with Beth's, like a rope. When she pulled her strand away, my loose end was frayed and useless. Losing Beth would transform my past, present, and future. What would I do with all of the memories—mostly happy ones— that I had collected with her over the past decade? They were too painful to dwell on, but if I tried to forget them, a substantial part of me would disappear with them. For that matter, who was I now, if I wasn't Beth's husband? When Beth left, she took with her my hopes of becoming a father, building a family, growing old with her; every vision for our future that I held dear. I could not fathom rebuilding my life without her at the foundation.

I also felt unbearably alone. As a boy, I lived with my family; in college, I lived in a fraternity; as an adult, I lived with Beth. But never in my life had I lived *by myself*. When Beth left, I lost my best friend and constant companion. For months, photos from our wedding day and other happier times enshrined the apartment, which was now "mine," not "ours." The hours and days seemed to go by *so slowly*. I dreaded coming home from work and the weekends (once the best parts of my week) because those times felt the strangest, passed the slowest, and gave me too much time to dwell on my pain.

I missed Beth's family—my family. After eight years of spending holidays, trips, and other gatherings together, I loved Beth's kin as my own. I admired her father as a model of kindness, reasonableness, and generosity; he introduced me to classic books and *The New Yorker*, and I introduced him to fantasy football and online chess. I would miss Beth's mother, with her positive spark and her creative spirit, who was as talented an artist as she was terrible at card games. I cherished Beth's sister, a social worker with a servant's heart, and her husband, with his easygoing nature and unassuming leadership; I counted both of them among my closest friends. Beth's niece and nephew were *my* niece and nephew; her grandparents were *my* grandparents; her cousins were *my* cousins. Except, of course, they weren't. Swiftly, along with Beth, they were gone, and I grieved the loss of every one of them.

On top of all of this, I felt heaps of shame and embarrassment. I had always attached a stigma to divorced persons, one of failure and desertion, and now I was about to join the club. I felt my divorce would be my scarlet letter. Others would see me as worthless, just like I saw myself, and no sensible woman would take a gamble on "used goods" like me, even if I could someday fall in love again—an outcome I highly doubted. Beth was a wonderful Christian woman. What would people think about me, or what would they assume I had done, when they heard Beth left me? The secondary realizations and questions—logistical, legal, financial—shook me like aftershocks. What will I do with my dogs? Will I have to hire an attorney? Should I stay in Chicago? It was all too much to wrap my head around.

I thought I had hit rock bottom. But for both me and my family, the hole was about to get much, much deeper.

CHAPTER 7

"I have been driven to my knees many times by the overwhelming conviction that I had nowhere else to go. My own wisdom, and that of all about me, seemed insufficient for the day."
—ABRAHAM LINCOLN

It was minutes before 8 a.m.—the start of Amber's scheduled work shift—on November 5, 2010, and Amber was just a few blocks away from Peel's Salon Services, the full-time sales job she held to support herself and her son Bailey. Amber had just dropped off Bailey at daycare. She now sat in her black Ford Explorer at a southbound stoplight, first in line, waiting for her signal to turn green.

More than 400 feet to Amber's left—according to several eyewitnesses—a 47,200-pound dump truck loaded with broken concrete barreled westbound in Amber's direction at 40-45 miles per hour when its light turned yellow. A certified accident reconstructionist later testified that the truck had twice the distance it needed to make a safe stop. But the driver did not brake; instead, he revved his engine and accelerated to beat the light, leaving in his wake a thick black plume of exhaust. With more than a football field's length to cover during the 3.7-second yellow signal, the truck had no chance of safely clearing the crossroads. The truck was at least 150 feet short of the intersection and still hurtling toward Amber at top speed when its light turned red.

Amber's signal flashed green. She stepped on the gas, blindly trusting that her way was secure. As the dump truck bore down on her, its driver did not honk, flicker his lights, or take any other action to alert Amber to his approach. In a crushing furious instant, the 23 ½-ton dump truck T-boned Amber's driver's-side door, folding her Explorer like an aluminum can and swallowing it whole in a shrieking, smoldering mass of glass and metal. Smoke burst from the truck's tires as the driver finally slammed his brakes, post-impact. The truck plunged through the intersection, Amber's Explorer wrapped around it, and slid to a stop in a nearby open field.

*   *   *

Dad got the call around 8:30 a.m. It was Mom, in a panic, relaying the news she'd just received from first responders: another daughter; another horrific collision; another apparent brain injury; and another emergency life-flight helicopter ride to the same hospital where Kayla died six years before. Dad was in Chicago at the time, trying to help me piece my life back together. He responded with a single shrill wail— *"NOOOooooo!!!"*—and then a series of frantic questions that Mom could not answer. Immediately, I hopped online and booked Dad on the next Omaha-bound flight—a Southwest Airlines departure leaving in a little more than an hour, with just one seat remaining. Dad hung up the phone and spit hurried explanatory sentence fragments at me as he collected his duffel bag, and then we ran together to the closest main street, where I hailed him a cab to Midway Airport. On his way there, Dad called friends from work and dispatched them to pick up Mom and bring her to the hospital, where he would meet her. I called Midway's airport security to alert them to the urgent circumstances.

Chicago's infamously bad traffic was gridlocked on Lake Shore Drive. On the phone with close friends, Dad wondered out loud if he might miss his flight. But as they prayed together, Dad's lane seemed to open before him, the traffic melting away as his cab scooted by bumper-to-bumper congestion in adjacent lanes. Airport personnel were ready for Dad the moment he arrived, and they swiftly whisked him to the front of a long security line and onto his flight, where the last seat on the boarded plane was waiting for him in the first row. As Dad stowed his bag in the overhead compartment, he glanced back to find seemingly every passenger in the plane looking at him, concernedly, wondering what might be wrong. Almost as soon as he sat down, the plane taxied from its gate. A flight attendant named Kristy crouched by Dad's side, touched her hand on his arm, and said "Give me your daughter's name. I am a Christian and will be praying for her during the flight." Minutes later, as the plane ascended, Dad looked up from his angst and saw the flight attendant sitting across from him eight feet away, head down, eyes closed, with her hands cusped upon her knees in prayer. Later, Dad said "Even though, in that moment, I felt more alone than maybe ever, I was not. God saw to it." The plane landed in Omaha, and as Dad deboarded, the flight attendant again assured him: "I will keep praying for your daughter on the rest of my flights today. *I will.*"

* * *

Back in Chicago, I sat alone on my couch, motionless, staring at the floor in a sort of trance for at least twenty minutes. For the first time in my life, I questioned my grip on reality. *Is this really happening?* Everything I was experiencing—first the separation from Beth, and then the news about Amber and the sudden flashbacks to Kayla's accident— seemed too shocking, terrible, and cumulative to be true. For a month, I had hovered at emotional extremes, eating infrequently and sleeping little. Might this just be an awful dream or hallucination, borne of my stress and fatigue, where the worst fates I could imagine all coalesced simultaneously? Taking a cue from the movies, I actually pinched my side and slapped my right cheek. *No. This is happening*—to me and to my family, again—*and I need help.*

I called my pastor, Phil, at Ravenswood Covenant Church. Like me, Phil lost a sibling (two, in fact) in a childhood car accident. He and I had been meeting for coffee regularly ever since Beth told me our marriage was over. Pastor Phil had a practical, disarming way of relating to me and dispensing wisdom, and over time I developed a genuine trust in and appreciation for him. When I told Pastor Phil what had happened to Amber, he dropped everything and came immediately to my apartment, arriving within minutes. We sat together at my kitchen table, allowing some time to pass in silence. After a long pause, he said, "Ryan, I wish I could say something to change the reality of this situation. But the truth is, no matter what happens to Amber—even if she comes through this—you and your family face a long, painful road ahead. God might not take away your burdens. But he *is* with you for the journey." Recognizing that his words could not calm or heal me, Pastor Phil suggested that we just ask God to speak to us. He picked up his Bible and rested it on the table along its binding and then parted his hands, allowing the Bible's front and back covers to flop down and its pages to cascade open—at random—to the book of Isaiah, chapter 43, from which Pastor Phil read verses 1-7 aloud:

> But now, this is what the LORD says—
>> he who created you, Jacob,
>> he who formed you, Israel:
> "Do not fear, for I have redeemed you;
>> I have summoned you by name; you are mine.
> When you pass through the waters,
>> I will be with you;
> and when you pass through the rivers,
>> they will not sweep over you.
> When you walk through the fire,
>> you will not be burned;
>> the flames will not set you ablaze.
> For I am the LORD your God,
>> the Holy One of Israel, your Savior;
> I give Egypt for your ransom,
>> Cush and Seba in your stead.
> Since you are precious and honored in my sight,
>> and because I love you,
> I will give people in exchange for you,
>> nations in exchange for your life.
> Do not be afraid, for I am with you;
>> I will bring your children from the east
>> and gather you from the west.
> I will say to the north, 'Give them up!'

and to the south, 'Do not hold them back.'
Bring my sons from afar
    and my daughters from the ends of the earth—
everyone who is called by my name,
    whom I created for my glory,
    whom I formed and made."

Pastor Phil repeated the passage, over and over, each time with a stronger voice and greater conviction. I buried my head in my arms and listened intently. With every repetition, I focused on a new fragment, saying it back to myself to internalize it:

"Do not fear."
"You are mine."
"The rivers . . . will not sweep over you."
"When you walk through the fire, you will not be burned."
"The flames will not set you ablaze."
"I love you."
"I am with you."

Gradually, like a slow drip, I felt a peaceful power building within me; it seemed to course through my veins and steady my racing heart. It felt like God was literally breathing into me strength that I could not summon on my own. When Pastor Phil finally stopped reading, I still felt gravely worried—about losing Amber, and about what that might mean for Bailey and the rest of us. I still had no clue where my life was headed, in the next year or even the next few hours. But I knew, to my very core, that whatever happened, and wherever I was going, I was yoked to God, and he was with me for the journey. And this was a very powerful thing.

Pastor Phil and I shared a prayer and then a quick lunch. I packed my bags, hoping to catch the afternoon flight to Omaha. Pastor Phil offered to drive me to the airport, but first we had to make a pit stop at church. When we got there, we learned that a church member who worked for Southwest Airlines, knowing nothing of my circumstances, had just dropped off for Pastor Phil five "buddy passes"—free roundtrip flights—in the off-chance that someone in the congregation might need them. My emergency flight home, and those that would follow in the months ahead, would be complimentary. An hour later, as my plane peeked through the clouds and into the bright November sky en route to my sister in Omaha, I felt God's promises repeating like a whisper: *"Do not fear. I am with you. You are mine."*

* * *

I arrived at the hospital to find a too-familiar scene: Dad, leaning forward, hands folded over his child in prayer; Mom, running her fingers through her daughter's hair; a visible head injury on the right side of my sister's skull. Amber was in a coma, completely unresponsive. Her complexion was pale and her skin cool to the touch. The front of her scalp was shaved, with an orange-brown antiseptic gauze caked around the metal rod that doctors had drilled into her head to measure intracranial pressure. Amber's CAT scans revealed deep bruising and bleeding in the right side of her brain as well as an alarming four-millimeter "midline shift"—essentially, the accident's impact moved the center of Amber's brain about a half-centimeter to the right, putting disproportionate pressure on certain parts of her brain and creating open space in others. There was more: a lacerated spleen, kidney, and liver; broken ribs and a collapsed left lung; and fractures all along Amber's spine, from her lower-back up through her neck.

We sat by Amber, listening to the pulses of the machines that monitored her and had assumed responsibility for her basic life functions, like breathing, which Amber's brain and body could not regulate. Given our experience with Kayla, and the similarities between my sisters' injuries, it was very difficult for me to remember and believe that a different outcome was possible this time around. While praying for the best, I could not help but contemplate the worst. *What if Amber dies?* In the past year, Amber had finally started to reclaim her life and self-worth, leaving behind her painful past, getting more involved with her church, and joyfully embracing motherhood. There is never a "right" time for a young person to die. But the timing of Amber's tragedy, just as things were turning around in her life, seemed especially cruel. *What about Bailey?* My sweet nephew, who would turn three years old in just a few weeks, had already dealt with more turmoil as an infant and toddler than any child should endure. Amber was the best, most stable, and most important part of his life. How would her loss—which would essentially orphan him—affect Bailey at this tender age? It seemed so unfair to stack the deck against him this way. *How would my parents endure more devastation?* I had seen the toll Kayla's loss took on both of them, but especially my mother. Could she survive the death of another child? And if she couldn't, who would raise Bailey?

The hours passed late into Friday night with no change in Amber's status. Around 11:30 p.m., Dad's cell phone rang; it was from an area code he did not recognize. He was stunned when he answered—it was Kristy, the Southwest Airlines stewardess, calling at the end of her shift. (Dad had given her his business card.) She wanted Dad to know she had kept her promise: she had prayed for Amber throughout the day, during each of her flights. After Dad gave her an update on Amber's condition, Kristy asked him to put his phone on speaker and set it on the bed next to Amber. Then she offered a beautiful, passionate prayer, asking God to save my sister—whom she had never met.

The night passed into Saturday morning, and then the afternoon, and then the evening. We praised God for every hour that Amber survived. But after nearly two days since the accident, there was no discernible improvement in Amber's condition. Her intracranial pressure remained stable, but at dangerously high levels. Amber's body, which was cool to the touch when I first arrived, now ran feverish; her temperature was stuck at 102 degrees, even though she rested on a "cooling blanket" designed to chill her. I began to wonder if a fate worse than speedy death was possible. I feared Amber may persist for days, weeks, or months in an apparent state of brain death, forcing us to decide when to "let go" and compounding our inevitable grief. Late Saturday night, I knelt by Amber's feet and prayed for her safe passage through the night, kissed her forehead, and then left the hospital, whispering goodbye.

I stayed the night on the couch of some friends and then joined them for church the next morning. It was a bright, beautiful, unseasonably warm November Sunday, and throughout the service, I felt washed over by the same power and hope that had gripped me days earlier with Pastor Phil in Chicago—a calmness that had no logical basis, but which assured me, with trust I could feel: *I am with you; you are mine.*

After the church service, I walked to my car, checked my phone, and saw I had a missed message. It was my Dad, and his voice was filled with elation as he shared the breaking news: earlier that morning—Sunday morning, November 7, 2010—Amber's nurse performed a routine cognitive check, loudly and forcefully commanding Amber to move her fingers if she could hear her. Amber's medical staff had done similar tests every few hours in the preceding two days, with no response. But this time—for the first time—Amber slowly, but unmistakably, answered the call. Her fingers loosely clenched into a ball, and after a few seconds her right hand completed the gesture: *thumbs-up.*

CHAPTER 8

"He heals the brokenhearted and binds up their wounds."
—PSALM 147:3

I used to think being "in" a coma, and coming "out" of one, was like flipping on a light switch—the patient essentially rested in a trauma-induced deep sleep, and if she were fortunate enough to "wake up" from it, she would reclaim her old self in short order. But brain-injury recoveries seldom go this way. Usually, the road to recuperation is slow and uncertain, with a range of semiconscious stops along the way. One test doctors have developed to gauge brain rehabilitation is the "Rancho Scale," which uses a number of criteria to assess the patient's cognition, including her responsiveness to stimuli, orientation, appropriateness of verbalizations and actions, memory recall, and judgment. These evaluations, in turn, translate to a scale from 1 (lowest) to 8 (highest), with each stage representing a kind of sequential graduation in the patient's recovery. No two brain injuries are the same; survivors will progress at different rates, and they might "plateau"—that is, stop improving—at any stage in their rehabilitation.

For Amber, the thumbs-up hand gesture marked a big breakthrough: it demonstrated that she could hear us, process what we said, and direct her muscles to respond appropriately—good for the second stage of the Rancho Scale. But this tiny feat, after two days of waiting, also foreshadowed just how long and strenuous Amber's healing process might be, as she fought to reconstruct brain functions ranging from the basic to the progressively complex. Simply put, we had no idea whether, or when, we might see Amber open her eyes; or hear her speak; or help her relearn how to write, do math, or walk. What we *did* have, though, were the blessings of a deliberate sign from Amber; the hope and belief that, in time, more milestones might follow; and inspiration in the form of prayers and encouragement from the thousands of people who monitored Amber's recovery on local news and through Amber's CaringBridge website, where my family posted daily updates on her progress.

Early on, though, Amber faced another major obstacle. For nearly a week, a respirator squeezed oxygen into her lungs through a tube running down her trachea. Amber needed the machine to breathe, but its support came with a risk: ventilator-assisted pneumonia (VAP), an infection triggered when bacteria invade the lungs through breathing tubes, bypassing the respiratory system's natural filters. Essentially, the ventilator that breathed life into Amber's lungs was also a harboring vessel for germs capable of destroying them. Full-blown VAP can be fatal—some studies suggest that one-third to one-half of patients who contract it will die from it—but precise figures are hard to come by because those who develop the condition are often already at risk of death from other serious ailments.

With each passing day, Amber's medical team worked to wean her off of the ventilator. But by day six—as Amber's lungs became ever-more inflamed, with fluid accumulating in them—it was still unclear whether she could breathe on her own. The risk of prematurely "extubating"— removing the breathing tubes—was serious. Amber's throat was swollen from irritation, and her neck was rife with hairline fractures. If, upon having her respiration tubes removed, Amber was unable to breathe independently, then her doctors would have to scramble to reinsert them. In doing so, they could inadvertently damage her already fragile vertebrae or even sever her spinal cord, paralyzing her. On November 11, nearly a week after her accident, Amber's medical team determined that, despite their reservations, Amber had reached a tipping point where the risk of infection outweighed the risk of neck trauma. They removed Amber's breathing tubes. Below is my CaringBridge update summarizing what happened next:

This was a hard day for Amber. Until now, we hadn't seen any true setbacks. Sometimes Amber's progress was slower than we hoped for, but Amber never finished a day in worse shape than she started it. We can't say that of today.

Things started well enough: around 10:30 a.m., Amber's doctor authorized the removal of her breathing tubes. We'd been anticipating this decision for days. The doctor wasn't certain Amber was ready and described his decision as "aggressive," but the whole team thought it was time to try. The extubation was complete an hour later, and we were cautiously celebrating this important milestone.

Amber's breathing tubes were replaced by an oxygen mask, which was strapped to her face. Right away it appeared her breaths were shorter and more spasmodic than they had been with the tubes. This is not uncommon after an extubation, but it was a situation that required monitoring. Among other things, we kept a close eye on Amber's oxygen saturation levels (the amount of oxygen making it into her bloodstream) and her breathing volume (deepness of breath).

Around 3 p.m., Amber's doctor determined that the breathing tubes needed to be reinserted. Her breathing volume wasn't satisfactory, and she wasn't responding to verbal commands. This was partly a preventative decision, as we couldn't risk having to deal with a breathing emergency in the middle of the night.

As discussed in earlier journal entries, the possibility of having to reinsert the tubes was the biggest fear in removing them. Amber's throat was swollen, which made intubation difficult. Even more concerning were Amber's neck fractures. Ideally, the breathing tubes are inserted by drawing the patient's neck back as far as possible (think of sword swallowing). Amber's neck fractures required the doctors to keep her head perfectly set while she lay down, then the tubes had to be jimmied down her throat until the doctors found their way to the top of her lungs.

While this was happening, Amber couldn't get oxygen (her mask was removed and the tubes were not yet in place). Her oxygen saturation levels fell below 80%, which is roughly akin to a normal person holding her breath for as long as she can. Oxygen deprivation can cause brain damage, but the doctors think Amber's saturation remained high enough, and the deprivation was short enough, that she avoided any additional brain damage.

Even with the breathing tubes back in place, we were not out of the woods. During the intubation procedure, Amber's central line IV (which was inserted in her left-upper chest) was knocked loose, so she needed to have a new IV inserted, this time in her right-upper chest. During this procedure, Amber's heart rate suddenly skyrocketed to 240 beats per minute. For the sake of comparison, a normal resting heart rate is between 60-100 beats per minute, and a nurse told me that his heart rate got up to 195 beats per minute when he went skydiving.

The medical team was immediately concerned about this development. They called a pharmacologist, who quickly arrived and injected Amber with a fast-acting heart medication reserved for serious emergencies. Thankfully, it worked, and within a few minutes Amber's heart rate had fallen to about 160.

All told, right now Amber is in about the same condition as she was in three days ago: she is being sedated through her IV, her breathing tubes are in, and her responses to verbal commands are slow. This is a setback given Amber's recent improvements and our optimism in having the breathing tubes removed.

With that being said, we knew this process could be slow, and that not every day would bring progress. Nothing that happened today necessarily affects the chances of Amber's long-term recovery. We will remain hopeful in Amber's recovery.

With love,
Ryan

*   *   *

Over the next few days, Amber's progress seemed to sputter and stall. But my parents did not fret. Their daughter was alive! They celebrated Amber's every achievement, no matter how small—for instance, when she first fluttered her eyelashes; when she tensed her feet as her neurologist tickled them with the prickly end of a broken popsicle stick; when she dutifully raised two fingers, and then three, on command. With love for their daughter and hope in God, my parents were willing to be patient. In the meantime, though, they longed to comfort Amber and hold her close—a simple task made difficult by the delicate web of tubes, braces, and machines that canopied her. But one must never underestimate a parent's capacity for ingenuity when it comes to loving his or her daughter, as my Dad captured in this excerpt from one of his CaringBridge journal entries:

With bed rails, pipes and tubes, it is hard for me to get near Amber. This is painful because all I want to do is hold my little girl. Yet God is so good here, too. I discovered last night that if I come around the very top of her bed, between it and the wall, I can lay my head on her pillow, 180 degrees the direction of hers, yet, next to hers. This also allows me to lay my hands on both shoulders and mimic a hug without touching her neck brace. It is priceless to me as a father.

*　*　*

It was November 16, Thanksgiving was soon approaching, and Bailey was just two weeks shy of three years old. He had not seen his mother in eleven days. Initially, our plan was to bring him to the hospital as soon as Amber's breathing tubes came out and the scene was less menacing, but now it was unclear when that might be. At first, Bailey seemed to enjoy his extended play-cation, staying primarily with my Aunt Kelly, who runs a daycare from her home. But as time passed, Bailey's disjointedness from his mother's absence grew, along with the frequency of his cries for her. We decided it was time for Bailey to meet with the hospital's pediatric counselor, who would help us determine whether and how to introduce him to Amber. I summarized that visit in the following CaringBridge journal entry:

> The medical news is mixed today: Amber's right chest tube (which stabilized her lung) was removed, but we also learned that Amber was developing "a little bit of pneumonia" in her lungs. I thought this sounded like getting "a little bit pregnant," but apparently pneumonia is a condition that comes in degrees, and Amber's case, for now, is slight. As noted in earlier posts, pneumonia is a common consequence of prolonged reliance on breathing tubes. Amber will be treated with antibiotics, but if her condition doesn't improve, we may have to consider non-intubation breathing options like a tracheotomy (a procedure in which an incision is made in the neck and a

breathing tube is inserted directly into the trachea, allowing the patient to breathe without using her nose or mouth).

Bailey came to the hospital late this afternoon and met with a pediatric counselor. First, the counselor explained that his mommy had "owwies." He said he knew that but "I don't know what happened!" The counselor gave him a cloth doll and asked him to show her what owwies looked like. Using markers, Bailey colored the doll. The counselor explained that mommy had owwies on her head, her hand, and her leg. She also explained that Amber was getting medicine that made her very tired.

Then she gave Bailey a small bag of toy medical equipment, and we examined each toy to show Bailey how it worked. After this, the counselor pulled out a larger bag of some real equipment that was "helping mommy," including breathing tubes and a neck brace. We transitioned from this to showing Bailey actual photos of Amber, pointing out the equipment that he now recognized. He was pretty attentive throughout.

Finally, we let Bailey pick out a stuffed animal for Amber and asked him if he wanted to give it to her. He said yes and seemed to be handling everything well, so we decided to bring him into Amber's ICU room.

Bailey was pretty timid upon first seeing Amber. We asked him if he wanted to tell Amber anything, and he shook his head no. He quietly watched as we talked to Amber and held her hand. After a few minutes, he said he wanted to leave. I walked out with him, but then he demanded that everyone leave Amber's room. I played with him in the hall for a minute, and then he announced he was ready to go back in.

This time he was more active—he touched Amber's hand, kissed her head, and told her to "wake up!" We explained she was just so sleepy, and he repeated "mommy's tired."

Taking advantage of the situation, Bailey saw some treats in the room, asked Amber if he could have one, and then informed us that "mommy says it's OK." (He scored a second snack with the same line minutes later.)

Amber showed small signs of responsiveness while Bailey was here. She moved her legs a bit, put up two fingers, and was able to get a slight grip when we tried to hold her hands. Bailey seemed amused whenever Amber moved, as if maybe she was just pretending to be asleep. He also helped put some lotion on her hands, which we explained helped heal the owwies.

Bailey never cried or seemed scared. Altogether, this visit went about as well as it could have. Thanks to all of you who shared insight on how to handle this sensitive event, and to the outstanding counseling team that worked with us today.

With love and thanks,
Ryan

Bailey's visit seemed to provide the spark Amber needed for her recovery to take root and progress. Because the next day, Amber opened her eyes widely and kept them open for fifteen minutes, staring blankly at nothing in particular before closing them for the remainder of the day. Two days after that, Amber's medical team removed her breathing tubes, again. But this time, the tubes *stayed* out, and Amber breathed, for the first time since her accident, normally and without assistance. By then,

I was shuttling between Omaha and Chicago almost every week. After several days' worth of hearing about Amber's steady improvements while I was away, I came back to Omaha and wrote the following update on Amber's CaringBridge site:

> Hi everyone, it's Ryan again, back with Amber after a short week in Chicago.
>
> Being away for five days has given me a unique ability to see how Amber has progressed. Most notable are the eyes: when I left, the best we'd seen was some fluttering; now they are open and blinking more often than not when visitors are around. And at times, Amber appears to be tracking movement or searching the room with them. In one sense, it's strange to see. When Amber's eyes were closed, she simply looked asleep. But now that they're open, we mostly just see a blank-looking stare. But there are some clear signs that Amber perceives her surroundings, so overall this is a very positive development.
>
> This morning we received an enthusiastic call from Amber's physical therapist, who had just finished an encouraging session with Amber. Here are some observations the therapist reported:
>
> *The PT helped Amber apply lip gloss and then told Amber she missed a spot. Amber lifted the wand (I have no idea if that's the right word) to her lips unassisted and reapplied the gloss.
>
> *The PT helped Amber wipe her lower face with a cloth, then told Amber to wipe her forehead, which Amber did by herself.

*The PT put perfume in Amber's hand and helped Amber's finger press the pump to spray it. Then the PT removed her hand, and Amber pressed the pump again on her own.

*The PT asked Amber what color her eyes were. Amber's mouth sputtered a "b" sound, which the PT thought could have been brown or blue. (Amber's eyes are brown.) Either way, Amber tried to speak.

Amber's therapist was clearly excited about these developments and referred to Amber as our "little miracle girl." It's great to hear that from a professional. She explained that in the past week, Amber has moved to a "3" on the Rancho scale that assesses levels of coma. To get to a "4," we'll look for signs that Amber is aware of what has happened to her. We're already seeing some of this, as tonight Amber has been touching her face and running her fingers over the part of her scalp where the pressure rod was inserted immediately following the accident.

This afternoon Bailey woke up from his nap crying for his Mom. I sat him on my lap and held him as he repeated a few times "I need my mommy!" Then he rested his head on my chest, still taking deep breaths. It was a tender moment. Then I felt a quick burst of pressure on my leg, and Bailey looked up laughing: "Did you heard my toot?!" Tender moment over.

We are so encouraged by Amber's improvements, which might result in her movement to a rehabilitation center by Thanksgiving. Two weeks ago, this hope seemed so distant.

Thank you all for your love, prayer, and support.

Sincerely,
Ryan

*　　*　　*

It's a strange thing, watching a loved one fight for her life while feeling so down about the value of your own. *Look at Amber*, I thought— *she's 25 years old, and nothing is guaranteed for her.* Yes, my wife left me, and that was devastating. Yet I still had so much—most glaringly, my health. Why couldn't Amber's setback give me the perspective I needed to appreciate what I had and move forward? But I simply . . . *couldn't.* My looming divorce had planted me in an emotional quicksand, and the harder I tried to will myself out, the deeper I got. At a certain point, I even started to feel badly *about* feeling badly—that is, I was ashamed of my own depression, weakness, and self-centeredness when I knew Amber had lost so much more than I, yet she continued to fight for her life. But then, kicking yourself over the way you feel isn't exactly a recipe for turning things around.

In the months following Beth's departure, I experienced every stage of grief, but denial was the leg that lingered the longest. Relying on two notions I believed to be true—(1) God can do anything, and (2) God desires to heal my marriage—I prayed ceaselessly for God to change Beth's heart and save our relationship.

In most states, a divorce can be either uncontested—where the husband and wife agree to dissolve their union together—or contested, where one spouse's refusal to "sign the papers" forces the divorcing spouse to formally sue the other for marital dissolution through normal legal channels, a process that can take years. Early on, I decided I would not voluntarily sign away my marriage. For me, there was symbolic importance in the distinction between *Beth* divorcing *me* (a phraseology that acknowledged the outcome was not my choice) and "getting divorced" (a turn of words that I felt made me an equal partner in the decision). I also felt, both in my heart and based on my reading of scriptures, that divorce—at least in our circumstance—was plain wrong. I knew I had made a vow, a solemn promise, both to Beth and to God. She (or eventually, a judge) could break that vow and take my marriage from me, but I would not just give it away.

In truth, though, I also had a less noble reason for refusing to cooperate: holding out gave me some semblance of control over an awful life-changing process that had somehow spiraled away from me. Until a court of law said otherwise, Beth was my wife—which is precisely what I wanted; what I needed. If some foot-dragging was all I had to do to extend my marriage and possibly prolong our chances for reconciliation, then so be it. The problem with my plan, I found (besides the fact that divorce battles are seldom fertile grounds for understanding and recommitment), was that as long as I kept hoping and praying for Beth to change her mind, then every new disappointment—Beth's gradual withdrawal from our every mode of communication; a harsh letter from her attorney; each next step in the legal process, no matter how predictable—pierced me anew. In other words, blindly believing that God would fix things required me to suspend reality. But every few days, and inevitably, reality slapped me in the face like a cold fish, crushing my morale all over again until I was ready to stand back up and repeat the cycle.

During this painful stretch, I dusted off an old devotional called *Grace for the Moment* by Max Lucado. It's a 365-page journal filled with Bible verses, anecdotes, and reflections for every day of the year. One day, the journal prompted me to read John 1:12: "To all who did accept him and believe in him he gave the right to become children of God." In the response section for that day, I wrote:

> Today I don't feel like God's child. I feel lonely. I feel
> desperate to be loved. I feel like a failure. I feel like I have
> no hope for happiness in this life. Today is a day when I
> need my father to wrap me in his arms and assure me he has
> a plan for me—that I will be OK. But how can I trust in

86

God's plan when I cannot see it? Wasn't God's plan for me
to be married to Beth? I feel so helpless right now.

Still, I kept praying for a miracle. As things looked ever bleaker,
with Beth divvying up our belongings, moving them out in chunks,
and signing a lease for her new apartment, I prayed ever more; it was
all I could do. Then, on November 22, 2010—just a few days before
Thanksgiving—I read the following daily devotional, which Lucado
titled "When God Says No":

> There are times when the one thing you want is the one
> thing you never get ...
> You pray and wait.
> No answer.
> You pray and wait.
> May I ask a very important question? What if God says no?
> What if the request is delayed or even denied? When
> God says no to you, how will you respond? If God says,
> "I've given you my grace, and that is enough," will you be
> content?
> *Content.* That's the word. A state of heart in which you
> would be at peace if God gave you nothing more than he
> already has.

In my response journal, I wrote: "What a passage to read after a
morning spent praying that God would save my marriage! God's grace
is intangible to me, but Beth's distance and Amber's health concerns are
present and crushing." "God, grip me with your grace," I pleaded, "and
help me to understand its sufficiency. Make my heart content with what
you have already given me."

Later, another daily devotional resonated with me. The focus
verse was James 5:16: "When a believing person prays, great things
happen." In the daily notes, Lucado writes:

> I believe there's great power in prayer. I believe God heals the wounded, and that he can raise the dead. But I don't believe we tell God what to do and when to do it.
>
> God knows that we, in our limited vision, don't even know that for which we should pray. When we entrust our requests to him, we trust him to honor our prayers with holy judgment.

While pondering God's great goodness and power, and my own "limited vision," I started to wonder whether a protracted legal battle with my wife was really what was best for us, or what was honoring to God. Maybe instead, it was time for me to face my fears of loss and loneliness and stop flailing about in a fruitless attempt to control this process. Maybe it was time for me to stop trying to stamp my own life vision onto God's blueprints. Maybe it wasn't healthy or honorable, but actually rather selfish, for me to force Beth to be in a technical relationship she no longer wanted to be a part of. Maybe I needed to let go and just trust God. That day, in my journal entry I acknowledged that God's vision of "great things" in James 5:16 may not be the same as *my* vision for greatness. "Thank you God," I wrote, "for playing out your promise of great things for me—even if not the way that I wanted (as with Kayla, and now Beth). Help me to trust your plans for me."

Throughout this journey, God gave me glimpses of hope to sustain me through the hardest days. One came in the person of Rev. George Moore, the senior pastor at West Hills Church in Omaha. Like me, "George"—as he insisted everyone call him—went through an unwanted, unexpected divorce as a young man. But months into his separation, and while he was still locked in heartache, George attended a Young Life Christian ministry conference, where he met a woman named Pam. Exactly one year later, in a blessing that exceeded George's wildest hopes and dreams, George and Pam were married—as they remained when I met George 22 years later.

George came into my life in a seemingly random way: days after I read and underlined a passage in *The Imitation of Christ* (a centuries-old book of prayers and recitations) discussing the virtue of "taking counsel with a wise and conscientious man," I walked into George's church on a snowy Omaha Sunday morning, knowing no one in the congregation and just hoping to worship in anonymity. Little did I know, George would soon become one of my life's greatest mentors and friends. George was caring, humble, funny, wise, and never too busy for me. Once, I called George from Chicago on a Sunday afternoon, sobbing, because seeing all of the beautiful children perform in my church's Christmas recital made me realize I might never have kids of my own. George lightened my mood by telling me about the time during *his* divorce when he heard a country song about a dying dog, and it made him cry so hard he had to pull over his car! More times than I can recall, I emailed George in a panic, sometimes saying only "Please pray for me right now" or "I don't think I can get out of bed today." Every time, George quickly got back to me with a thought or verse that calmed my heart. One day, George answered, "A good verse for you today is Matthew 11:28-30." ("Come to Me, all who are weary and heavy-laden, and I will give you rest . . . For my yoke is easy, and my burden is light.") Another time, George responded, "I will pray for you right now—in the meantime, go meditate on Psalm 46:10." ("Be still, and know that I am God . . . ") Usually, I am not the type whose nerves can be calmed by a verse-of-the-day, but George had a special way of reaching me—likely because I knew he had walked my path; he had found peace, hope, and love on the other side of divorce; and he was willing to walk that path, again, but this time as my guide.

Another unlikely source of hope emerged from Beth's Facebook page during one of my worst lows. I was in Omaha, by Amber's side at the hospital, wrapping up another CaringBridge entry. I signed onto Facebook and peeked at Beth's profile, which by then (around mid-November, six weeks into our separation) was among my few remaining links to Beth's life. What happened next was one of my many "cold fish" reality checks: I discovered that Beth had removed from her profile every "us"-related image—photos of me, photos of me and Beth, our dogs, Halloween parties, graduations, service projects, church events, family gatherings, vacations, *everything*—more than eight years' worth of memories. Looking back, it seems strange that some Facebook tweaking could hurt me so badly. But at the time, it felt like such a stark, palpable embodiment of Beth's determination to erase me from her life that I was overwhelmed with grief.

I bit down on a nearby hand towel and doubled over crying, trying hard not to make audible sounds so close to Amber. When I finally composed myself, I sat up straight, took some deep breaths, and wiped away my tears. As my watery eyes came into focus, they honed in on a tiny, thumbnail-sized photo smiling at me from the corner of Beth's Facebook profile. It was Jenny Stephenson, a "Mutual Friend."

Now, if you ask five people to describe their standards for who qualifies as an acceptable "friend" for Facebook purposes, you'll probably get five different answers. Some are ultra-conservative, only accepting friend requests from those they actually consider their close friends in "real" (and by that I mean "offline") life. On the other end of the spectrum are those who "friend" like it's their job, indiscriminately blasting requests to anyone or any*thing* with a profile. One of my real-life friends has a sensible, middle-of-the-road policy. When she receives a friend request, she asks herself: "If I saw this person at Walmart, would I say hello?" If the answer is yes, she accepts the request; if not, she rejects it. Generally, I lean liberal on Facebook-friend policies: to accept a request, I don't demand that the person actually be my friend; in fact, I don't even demand that I *know* the requester. Instead, I usually accept as long as I think the requester *genuinely believes that he or she knows me.* It's my way of being inclusive, and not wanting anyone to feel rejected. If we went to the same high school, or college, or once lived in the same city and have 25 mutual friends, *you're in!*

Whatever Jenny Stephenson's policy may have been, it is not completely clear when, how, or why she and I became Facebook friends. A few things *were* clear: first, we did not know each other, had never even met, and in fact had never had any communication of any sort, even on Facebook; and second, based on my loose friend policy, and Jenny's apparently strict one (my Facebook friends outnumbered hers 5-to-1), it was almost certainly *I* who friended *Jenny*, not the other way around.

In a teary-eyed, curious stupor, I clicked on Jenny's photo and navigated to her profile, quizzically thinking to myself *"Who is this?"* By our mutual friends, I could tell Jenny was a Nebraska graduate and a Greek-system alumna (which is how she knew Beth); by her status updates, I could tell she was a Chicago Bears fan (anti-Packers quips), a Christian (Bible verses and Rick Warren quotes), and very funny, in no particular order; and by her profile photos, I could see she had a dog, a perfect smile, and long eyelashes framing pretty, soulful light-brown eyes.

Oh no, I realized, as I scrolled through all 48 of Jenny's profile photos for the third-straight time. *I am becoming a Falker!* (A Facebook stalker.) I logged out and closed my laptop, a little bothered by what felt like—*could it be?*—the earliest inklings of a crush? It all seemed so strange—like I had accelerated from an emotional zero (bawling over my soon-to-be ex-wife) to sixty (feeling a spark of interest for someone else for the first time in nearly a decade) in 4.2 seconds. Given my fragile state, it was easy to question myself. But over the next few days, as I confided this sequence to friends, I took solace in their universally optimistic reaction. "Ryan, this is great news!" everyone said. "Allowing yourself to imagine a new life—one that is different from the one you expected, but nonetheless exciting—is a *huge* part of moving forward." "This isn't necessarily about Jenny Stephenson," they said—although to me, it was at least a little about Jenny Stephenson—"It's just about finding hope that you can be happy again, whatever that may ultimately look like."

* * *

On Thanksgiving Day, 2010, I was anguishing through another near-rock-bottom stretch. That morning, I helped prepare stuffing and mashed potatoes at a soup kitchen in Lincoln with a close friend, and when he hugged me goodbye, I broke down crying. From there I drove to Madonna Rehabilitation Hospital, where Amber had been transported from the Med Center two days earlier. Some of my former fraternity brothers' families had prepared and dropped off an incredible Thanksgiving meal for my family and me. Although Amber was unconscious and still eating through tubes, she was alive and with us, and we knew we had much to be thankful for. For my part, though, I was surrounded by loved ones, but still felt so alone.

Right before we ate, I suffered another Facebook-induced "cold-fish slap" moment. Earlier that morning, I had posted a Thanksgiving note on Facebook sharing my Kayla cell-phone story and some things I had learned about prayer and disappointment through two sisters' accidents. As I read through the encouraging feedback my Facebook friends had posted about my note, Beth suddenly popped up as a "Suggested Friend"—which was surprising in itself (because until then, we had remained Facebook friends), but this time it was under her *maiden* name. Beth's former profile—the one where she and I still shared a surname, at least nominally—was gone, along with my last reliable connection to her. I cried, again—an ugly, uncontrollable cry that even my cousins could not escape—and then I made a decision. I could not endure another year or more of fighting for my marriage in court. It was not healthy or right for me to draw out this pain. I loved Beth, but I would let her go—I would sign the divorce papers.

I asked for some time alone. Then I prayed to God, asking him to help me trust in his vision for my life and to walk with me through whatever lay ahead. Hard as it was, as I prayed, I experienced (much to my surprise) some relief—like a weight being lifted off of my shoulders. Or maybe more like a Band-Aid being ripped off. I could let go of my restless waiting for the next sad surprise. God still had a plan for me. It just wouldn't be my plan.

When I finished praying and looked back up to my laptop screen, I saw I had a new Facebook notification. Someone else had commented on my Thanksgiving post.

It was Jenny Stephenson.

CHAPTER 9

"Because of the Lord's great love we are not consumed, for his compassions never fail. They are new every morning; great is your faithfulness."
—LAMENTATIONS 3:22-23

In February 2010—about nine months before we "met" on Facebook—Jenny ended a seven-year relationship with her fiancé when she realized, after considerable prayer and self-reflection, that it was not the unconditionally loving, spiritually uplifting, long-term plan God had for her. Even though it was Jenny's decision, she, too, felt the loss of life vision and companionship, newfound loneliness, and concern for her uncertain future that I would experience later that year. Jenny took up journaling, rededicated herself to prayer, and relied on the love and support of her friends and family to help carry her through the hardest early months. But the holidays sometimes have a way of sifting sad feelings to the top. By November, Jenny still had not dated anyone since her breakup, had no serious "prospects" on her radar, and was feeling increasingly antsy about God's plan for her life. One Sunday morning at West Hills Church—the same church where George pastored, and where, I later learned, Jenny had been a member since her childhood—George encouraged churchgoers to jot their prayers and concerns on 3" x 5" index cards enclosed in their bulletins, walk to the front of the sanctuary, and lay them at the altar. This was a fairly common calling at West Hills; George thought of it as a literal way for congregants to offer their anxieties to God and trust him to answer their prayers in his way and time. That morning, as Jenny prayed, God laid messages of patience, trust, and obedience on her heavy heart. She pulled out her index card and wrote: "Lord, please help me to not feel loneliness, but <u>hope</u> that the person you have for me will come into my life when <u>you</u> see is right." Jenny set her index card on the altar, beneath the cross, symbolically giving her burdens to Jesus and completing her prayer—*Amen.*

As Thanksgiving approached, God seemed to be laying at Jenny's feet a request of his own. Jenny was a prototypical introvert: shy in new groups, more comfortable listening than talking, and happier to spend a Friday night at home with a close friend, her dog, and pizza than in a crowded bar double-fisting margaritas. Her tight-lipped nature also defined her faith, though: Jenny had *never* prayed out loud (ever!), and she seldom discussed spiritual matters even with those she trusted most, let alone among more casual acquaintances. But for the past few weeks, as Jenny journeyed—at George's recommendation—through Rick Warren's "The Purpose Driven Life" (a 40-day guide to discovering one's spiritual identity and purpose), she felt God tugging her out of her comfort zone and into a more active, deliberate faith. On Day 31, "Understanding Your Shape," Warren describes how the reader's unique experiences— and in particular his or her most *painful* experiences—also provide the greatest ministry opportunities. The Bible says that God "comforts us in all our troubles *so that we can comfort others.*" (2 Corinthians 1:4) In other words, Warren writes, "God intentionally allows you to go through painful experiences to equip you for ministry to others." While this message was still brewing within Jenny, Warren drove it home later that week, emphasizing on Day 35 how our biggest fears, our deepest hurts, and the things we're "most reluctant to share" are "the very tools God can use most powerfully to heal others." In her book, Jenny highlighted these messages in pink, along with another passage imploring her to let others "find healing in your wounds." After all, Warren reasoned, when we "weave the weak strands of our lives together, a rope of great strength is created."

It was in this spirit, amidst this new personal challenge, that Jenny reached out to me, a stranger, on Thanksgiving day. She first heard Amber's story on the ten o'clock news and had since then followed it on CaringBridge and Facebook. When Jenny read my Thanksgiving post, she later told me, she felt a "whisper," something "nudging" her to reach out and encourage me, despite her strong usual inclination to keep to herself. "Ryan, you are filled with wisdom and strength!" Jenny commented on my Facebook note. "What a gift you share with the world!" *Whew!* I thought with a flood of relief after I checked my new Facebook notification and read Jenny's comment. (At first, I feared Jenny had somehow found out about my Facebook-stalking and was calling me out on it publicly.) Hours later, when my resting heart rate was finally within normal ranges, I messaged Jenny to thank her for her kind words. Jenny felt the same spirit-filled compulsion, born in her Purpose Driven Life reflections and reinforced with a whisper, when she went out on a limb and responded again—this time sharing with me the personal trials and spiritual growth she experienced through her breakup earlier that year, in hopes that it might encourage my family and me as we journeyed alongside Amber.

My mind was blown. Before this exchange, for all I knew Jenny might be in a serious relationship, or even engaged. For all *she* knew, *I* was happily married. But by praying for God's guidance, making herself vulnerable, and following the nudges, Jenny started a conversation that kicked off a friendship. To be sure, it was an emotionally complicated arrangement; I was still in the throes of a devastating divorce that I had only recently begun to accept, and Jenny (unbeknownst to Jenny) had played a not-insignificant role in helping me start to believe I could someday have feelings for another woman. But more than anything, I felt blessed by this new unlikely Facebook-based camaraderie. After she learned of my separation, Jenny openly shared her own recent grief journey with me, and in doing so she gave me hope that I, too, might someday enjoy happier times. Early on, Jenny encouraged me by sharing a journal entry she wrote almost six months after she broke off her engagement, reflecting on how far she'd come by trusting God:

> I am feeling very appreciative of my blessings today. I am
> on the other side of my dark cloud and feeling very proud.
> With God at my side, I faced and conquered a lot.

He infused me with the strength and self-worth to open my eyes to the relationship I was in. He reminded me that seeing and facing the truth is the only way to feel happiness. Most of my prayers early on were for just that. I needed to know I would be OK no matter what happened. I was fearful of being alone (single). I was fearful of losing a seven-year relationship. I was fearful of what it would show me inside myself. I didn't feel like I had the strength inside me to take the more difficult path. These thoughts and fears were what I prayed about in the beginning.

I knew He had answered my prayers when I felt His energy and strength inside me. I felt His hand on my shoulder, reassuring me that it would be OK no matter what. He promised me that He would take care of me. He promised me that it would all be worth it, but I would have to trust Him and ignore my fears. He assured me it would be a difficult road, but He would not leave my side for one moment. He assured me I would not be alone. He assured me that no matter how sad I felt or how hurt I was, He would be there to listen and understand. He assured me that I could trust him with whatever I was feeling and He would show me the right way.

There were many nights I laid in bed crying heavily feeling lost and confused about what my future would be. I could almost visualize these two very different roads, and I had no clue which one I would be taking. They were so dramatically different. Standing at a crossroads like this was daunting. I felt uneasy and confused often. I felt so attached to this person and this relationship. I didn't know what I would be or do without them.

I was scared to admit this relationship had failed. I was scared of the embarrassment of calling off my wedding. I didn't want to be single again. I didn't want to start over again. God helped me to see that these things were only external variables. They had nothing to do with the relationship working. They had no place in my decision making. I knew He was right, so I did my best to ignore and rise above these fears when they came up. If I should have to deal with them later, then fine. He and I would deal with it then. I had the confidence to look those fears in the eye and say "So what?"

I feel so fortunate to have been able to set aside my worries and fears to trust Him completely. That is what got me through the dark nights and difficult days—trusting His promises and considering them done. I was able to completely surrender to Him. I walked off the cliff and He caught me. I took the difficult path (and it was as difficult as He told me it would be) but I got through it. It's amazing how much you can endure when you know He is at your side. When He finally told me that it was OK for me to let go of this unhealthy relationship—which I had been fighting to save and clinging to for so long—I was relieved. I waited and He had given me an answer. I had the confidence to face whatever waited ahead, because He had come through for me. I knew together God and I could make it through anything. I knew I was finally on the path of truth.

I have this dream or image of God and I running together. I take His hand and we run full-speed ahead into the storm. My eyes are closed because it is so dark and rain is hitting my face. I can't see what is ahead or what way will get us out. It's hard to keep up. I am running beside Him gripping

His hand tightly, because I know He knows the way out. It is a feeling of complete trust and faith.

I am infinitely grateful for this challenge. It has shown me so much about myself and God. Before, I had only been taught or told of God's love and insight. But I had never felt these things so strongly from inside myself. It is life-changing to feel His love and security wrap around you. He was so patient with me and never left my side. For this, I will never allow the world to drown out His voice. I will never let go of His hand. I will always trust Him. When I feel myself drifting away, I will always go back to Him.

Days later, Jenny explained to me that our developing friendship felt to her like an opportunity to fulfill God's call to encourage those going through similar trials with our own experiences of his strength, patience, and faithfulness. Jenny wrote:

I smile because I believe God has orchestrated a great exchange. He has a way of piecing things together in a way we would never anticipate—all for the sake of a little hope. Another reminder to me that God is always whispering if we are tuned-in to hear Him. This world teaches us to conceal our pain and weakness, while God teaches us that sharing our pain and lessons is the best way to help one another. This is our purpose: "It is God Himself who made us what we are and given us new lives from Christ Jesus; and long ages ago he planned that we should spend these lives helping others." (Ephesians 2:10)

In my response note, I thanked Jenny for her openness and for the feelings of peace and new optimism it had given me, writing: "I hope one of these days I'll be able to join you on the other side of this dark cloud."

* * *

The outpouring of community (and, eventually, nationwide) interest in and support for Amber's recovery was overwhelming. A little more than a month after Amber's accident, her CaringBridge site had registered more than 200,000 visits. (Today, that figure tops one million.) After Thanksgiving, my Mom posted on CaringBridge, inviting readers to send us ornaments to decorate the seven-foot Christmas tree we put in Amber's room, with the hope that "Amber will look at these ornaments in years to come and know how many people prayed for her and love her as much as her family does." And so the March of Ornaments began: hand-crafted ornaments, battery-operated ornaments, family-heirloom ornaments, from Texas to Pennsylvania, Tennessee to California, Maryland to Utah—all told, more than 300 ornaments from nearly half of the United States. Many came with touching personal stories of lives impacted by our family's trials and Amber's recovery, often beginning "You don't know me, but . . . "

After she moved to Madonna Rehabilitation Hospital, Amber's progress came in fits and starts, always erratic, but always trending positively. For weeks, Amber's speech therapists pleaded with her to start answering questions "yes" or "no" instead of with a thumbs-up or down; inevitably, Amber slowly moved her lips, but she could not emit a sound. Heartbreakingly, on Bailey's third birthday—which we celebrated by Amber's side in Lincoln, with Bailey opening prewrapped presents purchased by Amber's friends at Peel's, all of whom insisted that Bailey's gifts come "from Amber"—Amber repeatedly mouthed "happy birthday" to her son, but her words were inaudible. That all changed with Amber's early-December breakthrough, which Mom gleefully captured in the following CaringBridge entry:

> On Tuesday, Craig and I stayed with Amber in Lincoln late into the evening. My sister, Kelly, was watching Bailey in Omaha, and they called us to say goodnight before she put Bailey to bed. Naturally, we put Bailey on speakerphone so

Amber could hear her son. After five consecutive minutes of Bailey talking (!), a break came in the conversation, and Amber seemed like she wanted to say something. We put the phone next to her face, and although it took every cell in her body, she whispered "I love you, Bailey."

Really.

We were in shock and started crying (as did the nurse's aide with us) and Bailey just simply replied "I love you too, mommy" and "Good job, mommy." This was the first time Bailey had heard his mommy's voice in over a month, and Amber looked extremely proud of herself.

I was so proud of Amber and am so in love with both of them.

Shelly

Slowly but surely, Amber continued to reclaim her cognitive, speech, and fine-motor skills. In his mid-December CaringBridge post recording Amber's advances, Dad's excitement was palpable:

Well, I don't know where to start ... Which miracle today do you want to hear about first?

I arrived at Madonna this morning as they were wrapping up the first physical therapy session with Amber in the gym. We visited with the nurse in her room and I put the bed railing down so I could sit near Amber. I then read her some cards and letters that had come in the mail.

Speech therapy was up next, and this part really surprised me today. First, the speech therapist pulled up a chair and held up a small writing board. She wrote a "B" on it and asked Amber to name a U.S. city beginning with that letter. Amber didn't respond until the speech therapist said "I can think of one on the coast known for a place called Fenway Park." To which Amber faintly whispered "Boston." BLEW ME AWAY. Next, the speech therapist repeated the exercise, requesting a city beginning with the letter "P" and then one starting with "O." After some more clues, Amber whispered "Philadelphia" and "Orlando," and I was further stunned.

The speech therapist then asked Amber to look at the Christmas tree and tell her which holiday is approaching. "Christmas" squeaked out. Next, "Amber, let's talk about different fruits. Name one that starts with the letter 'L' and some people put it in their iced tea."

A fragile "lemon" was barely audible, but the therapist's look told me I needed to be patient.

All of this absolutely made my morning and was entirely unexpected, but then something else happened a couple of hours later as I was telling Amber goodbye, needing to head back to Omaha for an afternoon of meetings.

I knelt down in front of Amber's wheelchair and told her I loved her; that I'd be back soon. She seemed to mouth something, and because it was going to be the last thing I heard from her that day, I really wanted to hear her. She then leaned towards me, near my left ear. While I'm expecting her to whisper something, she instead gives me a kiss on the side of my head! This received a loud "awwwwe!" from the nurse's aide. Again, Amber surprised me.

But the biggest surprise came around 4 p.m. when I picked up a voice message from Shelly saying "Call me right away; good news!" Hey, when your wife says to call her right away, you do it. ;-)

Shelly picked up on the first ring and told me she received a call about an hour earlier. When she answered, a voice said "Hi" and Shelly said, "Excuse me?" The voice on the other end repeated "Hi, Mom," and Shelly exclaimed "Amber . . . are you calling me?!" Amber had apparently motioned a nurse's aide for her phone and, with the aide's assistance, called her mother!

This is an "awe" day all right, but it's for God's infinite power and healing grace.

And, friends, go out and hug a therapist today. It doesn't matter who they are or where they work, just lock on and don't let go.

Craig

* * *

Still, Amber's progress often felt like three steps forward, two steps back. Amber sometimes tried to communicate with a pen and paper, scribbling nonsensical notes (and often missing her pad of paper altogether) that apparently meant something to her, but to no one else. Some mornings, Amber woke up without the will or ability to take on her full slate of scheduled therapy, refusing to go to "class," as she called the sessions. For a time, almost every visit started with Amber's repetitive, seemingly scripted set of questions: "What happened to me?" (You were in a car accident.) With wide eyes: "Is Bailey OK?" (Yes, you were alone in the car.) "I can't move my left leg—what is wrong with it?" (You injured the right part of your brain, which controls the left side of your body, but you are getting better.)

Sometimes, while she was fully awake, Amber asked me to help her "wake up." I told her I didn't understand. "Why can't I wake up?" she repeated. Then I got it: Amber was finally becoming alert enough to recognize and appreciate that she was not her "normal" self, but she didn't know why, and she couldn't do anything about it. To Amber, it felt like she was in a dream—perceiving her surroundings slowly, semi-cognizantly, and unable to think as clearly or move as readily as she expected. "Amber," I asked, "do you feel like you're dreaming?" "Yeah," she answered. "Can you just shake me so I can wake up?" I told Amber she was not dreaming, but it was normal for her to feel that way, because she was healing from a serious head injury. When I said this, Amber seemed paralyzed with dread that she would forever remain in a fog. To allay her fear, I analogized her head injury to a leg injury. When someone breaks a leg, I explained, he can't just walk on it the next week; it takes time to heal and rehabilitate. The same is true, I told Amber, of her brain: she wouldn't just wake up tomorrow and be back to normal. But over time, and with hard work, she would keep getting better.

* * *

Few things were clear to Amber. She frequently expressed confusion about her age (she thought she was 20; she was actually 25), her location, and the correct month and year. But on one point, Amber was lucid, consistent, and emphatic: on the day of her accident, she saw Kayla.

Accounts of near-death experiences—which typically consist of an awareness of potential death, feelings of intense peace and love, and the encountering of heavenly beings (often deceased loved ones, and often dressed in white), among other common characteristics—date back to the 4th century B.C., in Plato's The Republic. Although one Gallup poll suggested that as many as eight million people in the United States alone claim they have experienced a near-death experience, the topic remains misunderstood and somewhat taboo, especially in scientific circles. Often, the phenomenon is explained away as wishful thinking, or dreaming, or brain malfunctioning, although other medical experts argue that conditions of the brain and body alone cannot explain near-death experiences.

In *Proof of Heaven*, Eben Alexander, M.D., presents a stunning account of his own near-death experience. Beforehand, Dr. Alexander, a neurologist, was not particularly religious—he described himself as "a step above a 'C & E'er (one who only darkens the door of a church at Christmas and Easter)." Over the course of 25 years of medical practice, Dr. Alexander had often heard his own patients' near-death accounts, which he treated with worse than skepticism. After all, "[t]o be truly skeptical, one must actually examine something, and take it seriously." Instead, Dr. Alexander simply "knew" his patients' claims were impossible. "Like an ocean wearing away a beach, over the years my scientific worldview gently but steadily undermined my ability to believe in something larger . . . Belief would have been nice. But science is not concerned with what would be nice. It's concerned with what *is*."

That all changed in November 2008, when a rare, virulent form of *E. coli* bacterial meningitis ravaged Dr. Alexander's brain, pushing him into a six-day coma and onto the brink of death. While he was comatose, Dr. Alexander claims he experienced a vivid, fantastic, "ultra-real" state of consciousness: Heaven, where God's indescribable, infinite, and unconditional love flooded him, and where momentous understandings were distilled to Alexander intrinsically and absorbed more deeply and naturally than our human senses could ever capture. Miraculously, Dr. Alexander not only survived, but he recovered complete cognitive functioning—an outcome without medical precedent.

Part of what makes Dr. Alexander's account so fascinating is the nature and degree of his infection. As he notes, "bacterial meningitis is arguably the best disease one could find if one were seeking to mimic human death without actually bringing it about." This is because while

Dr. Alexander was in coma, the more primitive or "housekeeping" parts of his brain—those responsible for his breathing and heart regulation, for example—continued to function. But his neocortex—the part of the brain that controls perception, language and conscious thought, and which "every single brain scientist will tell you is responsible for the human side of me: well, that part was gone." Thus, the crucial feature of Dr. Alexander's near-death account is "the sheer, flat-out impossibility of arguing, from a medical standpoint, that it was all fantasy."

Dr. Alexander concludes that science, for all its successes, has compromised "the most crucial component of existence—our human spirit" by discarding notions of the soul, afterlife, God, and heaven as make-believe merely because they raised questions that "proved difficult to answer through conventional scientific means." Alexander pleads that science and spirituality *can* coexist, and that his own near-death experience showed him "that the death of the body and the brain are not the end of consciousness," but rather "human experience continues beyond the grave." Perhaps most importantly, life after death "continues under the gaze of a God who loves and cares about each one of us and about where the universe itself and all the beings within it are ultimately going."

This all may seem like an excessively thorough prelude to Amber's near-death account. Nonetheless, I include it in hopes of softening the innate skepticism some (myself included) might initially feel toward accounts of near-death experiences, and to recount my own reading on the topic since I first spoke with Amber about what she saw on the morning of her car accident. Certainly, near-death accounts can captivate us; the book *Heaven is for Real*, published in 2010, has already sold more than three million copies. But the maddening—and completely unavoidable—characteristic of near-death experiences is that they occur, by definition, in another person's mind, subjectively, and thus cannot be examined using traditional tools. Ultimately, whether the speaker is Dr. Alexander, Colton Burpo, or Amber Wilkins, the listener is left to study the substance of the message and the credibility of the speaker, and then to draw his or her own conclusions. Each new near-death account is either pure nonsense (through deceit or delusion), or among the most important truths ever spoken. There is no room in between.

Amber's near-death account of the moments following her accident is as follows:

> *I was lying on a stretcher in the helicopter. I could hear the engine humming and the blades chopping. As we were getting ready to take off, Kayla walked through the helicopter's open door. She was wearing all white. She looked just how I remembered her, except a little older, and with long, beautiful hair. Kayla stood over me, silently crying because my body was in such bad shape. She stayed with me for the entire flight to the hospital. When we got there, she leaned over and kissed me on my nose. Without using words, she told me I was going to be OK. "So happy" and "total comfort" are the best ways I can describe how Kayla made me feel. The whole experience was very real to me.*

As she emerged from her coma, Amber told us about her meeting with Kayla over and over, almost as soon as she could construct complete sentences. It is hard to overemphasize the otherwise-fleeting nature of Amber's memory during this period. For months, almost every time I saw Amber she asked me to describe to her, again, her accident, her injuries, and her prognosis. She was often confused about basic details concerning her life and present circumstances. Even today, Amber has no memories during a three or four-month span beginning in early October, about a month before her accident (the last thing Amber recalls is learning of my divorce news), through late 2010 or early 2011, when Amber vaguely recalls understanding she was rehabbing in Lincoln. But smack-dab in the midst of this mental haze, Amber painted a stark, matter-of-fact picture of her encounter with Kayla—an encounter which took place minutes after Amber absorbed a direct, driver's-side impact with a massive, speeding dump truck—and Amber's description of these events has remained sharp and unswerving since then.

Before her accident, Amber seldom talked openly about spiritual matters or the afterlife. So when she awoke from a coma insisting that Kayla comforted her during the helicopter ride to the hospital—and then adamantly and consistently defends the exact same account years later—I believe her. In fact, I think it's one of the most important truths I've ever heard.

*   *   *

By mid-December, I had decided my future was in Omaha, not Chicago. So piled onto everything else, I now had the added sadness, stress, and discombobulation of a job search, apartment-packing, and saying goodbye to my friends and home church in Chicago, which had been my rocks throughout the divorce. In our online correspondence, Jenny offered her condolences, saying "We don't know why, but a big life-changing circumstance like this happens for a reason," and "down the road, the purpose of this may be revealed." But altogether, these sudden life changes converged like a perfect storm for a depressing holiday season. On Christmas day, my *Grace for the Moment* book quoted Philippians 2:7: "He gave up his place with God and made himself nothing. He was born to be a man and became like a servant." In my journal, I begged God to make the gift of Christ's birth "real and tangible to me this morning" and to bless me with peace. "Fill my thoughts with hope in your plan for my life," I wrote. "I need you so much, God."

For two months, my online friendship with Jenny grew—generally, with Jenny checking in on me and offering spiritual encouragement every week or so, and with me responding numerous times within 24 hours. Sometimes, I allowed myself to wonder whether someday, something more might be in store for Jenny and me. OK, that may be an understatement. In truth, I had felt an inexpressible but unshakeable connection to Jenny since the day she first popped up on my Facebook screen—a feeling only reinforced by our improbable Thanksgiving introduction, with Jenny reaching out to me on Facebook and sharing her personal journey, unprompted. But other times, I doubted my discernment and self-worth, and I felt silly and pathetic for even entertaining the idea of a future with Jenny. Waiting has never been my forte, and I often felt desperate for validation that Jenny might feel the same way I did. But even stronger than these sentiments was my feeling that God was in this, and I could trust him to finish the job he started; whatever the plan, it was better in his hands than in mine. During this time, I constantly prayed:

> Lord, teach me to be patient—with life, with people, and with myself. I sometimes try to hurry things along too much, and I push for answers before the time is right. Teach me to trust your sense of timing rather than my own and to surrender my will to your greater and wiser plan. Help me let life unfold slowly, like the small rosebud whose petals unravel bit by bit, and remind me that in hurrying the bloom along, I destroy the bud and much of the beauty therein.

> Instead, let me wait for all to unfold in its own time. Each moment and state of growth contains a loveliness. Teach me to slow down enough to appreciate life and all it holds. Amen.

On January 21, 2011, I flew back to Omaha to see Amber, and Jenny and I finally met, for the first time, in person. Jenny, a dental hygienist, had read about Amber's oral health challenges on CaringBridge. (Amber broke several teeth in her accident, and her limited motor skills made teeth-brushing difficult.) As a gift, Jenny bought Amber a high-end electric toothbrush and offered to join me in Lincoln to show Amber how to use it. I summarized our visit in the following CaringBridge update:

> Today I saw Amber for the first time in about three weeks, and she was in fine form! Her afternoon started well when she saw we arrived with Arby's for lunch (she's always been a sucker for curly-cue fries). Ever the opportunist, Amber

quickly asked that we cancel her afternoon therapy sessions so she could concentrate on eating. Her pleas were denied, and Amber was forced to snack on her lunch piecemeal amidst a full slate of afternoon sessions.

Amber seemed to grasp and execute all that she was asked to do. A breathing specialist measured her inhalation strength and found it not significantly worse than an average woman's. With her occupational therapist, Amber slid a loose grip up and down a long pole using her left (weaker) arm. She actually said it was "too easy," so I lifted the pole several feet and made her work for it. With her speech therapists, Amber read out loud an article about Miss Nebraska being crowned Miss America, and she also made conversation about her family. It was the loudest I'd heard Amber speak, and it sounded more like actual talking than the whispering to which we've grown accustomed.

Amber also flashed some sass. When a nurse asked me when a change had been implemented into Amber's diet, and I said I didn't know, Amber waved her hand and asked why no one was asking her. When a speech therapist asked about Amber's "daughter," Amber said Bailey was her son, and "there's a big difference." (Amber then said it was easier to raise a boy than a girl, using herself and me as a case-in-point.) She also seized opportunities to embarrass me in front of my friend, Jenny, who accompanied me on this visit.

After the sessions, Amber wanted to work overtime: she asked me to quiz her memory. I asked a series of questions ranging from our former pets' names to her old address to the names of her former roommates, and she didn't miss one. Later, she showed some confusion, asking me how life in "the fraternity" was going (when I told her I hadn't lived in FarmHouse for years, she remembered right away) and expressing confusion about where she was. But overall, her mind seemed alert.

The highlight of the afternoon came when my friend, a dental hygienist, delivered Amber a Sonicare FlexCare electric toothbrush. This is the Rolls Royce of toothbrushes, and my friend is the Michael Jordan of hygienists: driven, skilled, and fiercely dedicated to her trade. (Side joke: What did the dental hygienist of the year get? Answer: a little plaque.) I couldn't help but laugh when Jenny brought out a full-mouth demonstration model and used it to show Amber how to use the brush, right down to the proper 45-degree angle to be applied along the gum line. Amber was so thankful for this very practical gift, which will help her maintain oral health while she regains dexterity in her hands.

Late in the afternoon, as we laid Amber in her bed before we headed back to Omaha, I recounted for her all of the great things she'd accomplished that day. She said "I do it for Bailey."

Altogether, today was a blessing for all.

Ryan

Tonight's Bible verse is in keeping with our dental theme: " . . . Open wide your mouth and I will fill it." (Psalm 81:10)

From January 31 through February 2, 2011, Chicago endured one of its worst blizzards in recorded history. It dumped nearly two feet of snow into fifty mile-per-hour winds, prompted the cancellation of 1,300 flights at O'Hare and Midway, and left 900 drivers stranded on Lake Shore Drive for as long as twelve hours. Throughout the blizzard, I was holed up in my apartment with Ronald, a homeless man who regularly attended my church, and whom I invited in to weather the storm with me. Together, we feasted on Hot Pockets and Eggo waffles as I packed for my move later that month. Ronald relished my piping-hot furnace and comfortable bedding, snoozing his way through each day.

Five hundred miles away, the same winter storm had snowed in Jenny, who was cooped up at her home in Omaha when she hopped online and accepted my Facebook-chat invitation. After about an hour of messaging, I was feeling inquisitive. I asked Jenny what prompted her, initially, to reach out and open up to me about her life experience. Jenny explained that it was a series of "nudges" or "whispers" from God. At first, "it was just little thoughts, like sharing with you my appreciation for your Thanksgiving note." Then, as we got to know each other, "I just waited until I felt that spirit again to write to you and share with you. So everything I have shared with you has been very real, authentic and spirit-filled. To me, it's something God has given both of us."

Then, Jenny flipped the questioning and asked why her outreach had resonated with me. With a fast-beating heart and a quick prayer, I spilled the beans: "The full answer is fairly complicated, but to keep it simple . . . I just felt *something* too, and I wasn't sure what it was." I continued: "I felt strongly drawn not only to your story, but to you individually. And my prayer all along (for myself) has been to be thankful for what you are to me, now—which is a fun, caring friend—and not to wonder whether my 'feeling' is something more than that."

There, I said it. Essentially, I'd given Jenny the grown-up version of the elementary-school note I once slipped to so many Suzies, Lindsays, and Sarahs: "I like you. Do you like me?" I crossed my fingers that Jenny's note would land better than its predecessors.

A long pause in the conversation followed. *One-one thousand, two-one thousand . . . seven-one thousand . . .* I gnawed on my right-index fingernail. *Oh crap, oh crap, oh crap,* I thought. *This was a mistake.* Ronald shifted restlessly from my couch ten feet away, apparently sensing the nervous tension even in his slumber. Fearfully, I retreated, typing: "I hope I didn't say too much there, and that I didn't sound too weird . . . I'm sorry if I did."

More waiting.

Finally: "Not weird at all," Jenny answered. I exhaled. Another pause.

Then, Jenny's priceless follow-up: "I kind of feel the same way."

CHAPTER 10

"There are only two ways to live your life. One is as though nothing is a miracle. The other is as though everything is."
—**ALBERT EINSTEIN**

The next month was a whirlwind. On February 24, 2011, Amber moved from Madonna in Lincoln to Quality Living, Inc. (QLI) in Omaha, a top-notch post-acute rehabilitation facility. For the first time in months, Amber was *not* in a hospital! Then, four days later, I moved back to Omaha, too, saying goodbye to my friends, church family, and job in Chicago. In different ways, it seemed that both Amber and I were moving home for the next phases in our recoveries.

As soon as I unpacked, I did what any rational person working through the tail-ends of multiple, severe, overlapping life crises would do: fly to Costa Rica! Along with my two closest friends from high school, I voyaged to Tortuguero National Park, a coastal rainforest reachable only by boat or plane. After nearly six months of nonstop anxiety and depression, it was just what I needed. Highlights of the trip included, in no particular order: kayaking and hiking in search of monkeys, turtles, crocodiles, poisonous frogs, toucans, and three-toed sloths; eating deliciously fresh fruit and drinking milk straight from coconuts; learning that my pasty-white skin is, for some reason, a highly sought-after beauty feature among Costa Rican women, who were not shy about asking me to pose for photos with them; trekking to the top of Poás, a 9,000-foot active volcano, and peering down into its smoky crater; getting swindled by a street vendor to the tune of $30 for an off-brand version of sunblock that caked and crusted onto our faces like a spa-mask treatment (imagine grinding up ten pieces of chalk and adding five droplets of water, and you'll be close to the consistency), but was completely useless against the sun; and helping a desperate ranchero track down and lasso his escaped "vaca loca" (crazy cow).

Shortly after I returned, my divorce was legally complete. By then it had been six months since Beth left me. Throughout that span, I had been seeing a counselor once or twice a week to help me sort through my feelings. But it was still hard to prepare myself for the eerie, heavy finality of signing the documents that would end my marriage. It felt like I was closing the book on one life and starting an entirely new one. In the immediate aftermath, I was in constant emotional disequilibrium, unable to gather my bearings in a sea of unfamiliarity: at my new apartment, my new law firm, church . . . Seemingly *everything* had changed. Yet at the same time, as Easter approached I found a renewed, tremendous strength in God, rooted in faith in and dependence on him like never before. For years, during the season of Lent, I had given up hot water in my showers. My discomfort served as a daily, chilling reminder of Christ's infinitely greater suffering on the cross. But that year, I added a new twist, capping off each cold shower with a magnificent, momentary burst of hot water. For me, the ritual became a metaphor for healing, and an even better image of God's love for me—a love which includes pain, but also hope; sacrifice, but also victory; Good Friday, but also Easter.

Besides covering me in his love during my life transition, God also infused me with an unbridled thankfulness for the future I hoped to build with Jenny. My bond with Jenny was unique in that despite (and perhaps because of) the dramatic, special circumstances that connected us, we both suspected we were "meant to be"—call it God's plan, our destiny—before we ever went on a date. Looking back, this sounds just as crazy now as it did then. At the time, I wondered: *Can I trust my feelings?* In the same way an insane person seldom realizes his delusions aren't real, a small part of me questioned whether my emotional compass, spun and rattled amidst my recent turmoil, could accurately gauge my own perceptions. My closest friends, too—while cautiously optimistic about developments with Jenny—had some understandable apprehension. After all, only a few months ago they had witnessed me bawling facedown on their floors; staring blankly into a bowl of soup as dinner passed in silence; insisting, adamantly, that I would never love again. Was this kind of turnaround safe, or even possible?

But no one was more concerned or had a greater stake in my emotional well-being than Jenny. She had no interest in "rolling the dice" with me or being my rebound relationship. When she was ready to love again—and she *was* ready to love again—she needed complete trust in her partner. She needed faith that it was real and hope that it would last forever. She knew she could uphold her end of that bargain, but it seemed awfully early for her trust me to keep up my end. For most of her life, Jenny had been classically risk-averse, preferring always to play it safe. In this case, though, there was little doubt that I was a risky bet: divorced, wounded, and in transition. But with a tugging from the depth of her heart, God whispered clearly to Jenny in a way logic could not: *This is the gift I intended for you—it is safe for you to receive it.*

Of course, the journey from pen-pal to soulmate is more than a formality. Heart tugs or not, we had a lot of work to do—together, and me individually—to build a strong relationship foundation, and to realize the full potential of the precious gift God had given us in each other. To this end, Pastor George was an absolute blessing. After I moved home, George bridged the divide between my crisis-management focused therapy in Chicago and my ongoing need for reflection in Omaha, becoming my close friend in the process. George and I met in his office every week to slog together through the hills and valleys I experienced in the months after my divorce. I was open with him about my growing love for Jenny, a member of George's congregation. Oddly, George seemed almost as excited as we were, and a whole lot less concerned about the details of our emotionally precarious circumstances—probably because they sounded a *lot* like the circumstances he found himself in when he met his wife, Pam, and he knew how *that* story turned out!

Still, George challenged me to painstakingly work through my "stuff": the things I said and did that undermined my relationship with Beth, regardless of any contributing mistakes she may have made. George and I talked through my stuff, made lists of my stuff, and came up with game plans to make sure my stuff would never infect and cripple my relationship with Jenny. After one of our meetings, George told me "I am proud of you, Ryan. You are doing great. And this thing God has given you and Jenny is so special—what a blessing." Then, George paused and grinned: "Now, just try not to blow it."

Joking aside, at times I worried I might actually blow it. Some days, the burns from my recent past still seared, and I doubted myself. "Why," I asked George, "does it still hurt like this? Is it wrong for me to date Jenny when I'm obviously not 'over' my divorce?" George smiled lovingly and leaned back in his chair, resting his feet on the space heater between us. He told me about the time, several years into his marriage to Pam, when Pam packed her bags for an out-of-state Young Life trip and waved goodbye to him. Suddenly and inexplicably, George felt overwhelmed with panic and grief. George knew Pam was just traveling for a few days, and she would come back home. But another, more primitive part of his brain sensed only *my wife is leaving me*, connecting the dots to the abandonment and despair he felt during his divorce. George was taken aback by how raw and combustible his emotions were, even years after the fact. "The point," George explained, bringing his anecdote back to me, "is that when Beth left, she took with her a piece of your heart that Jenny can never perfectly fill. Our hearts heal, but with bruises and scars." "The beauty," George said, "is that when we acknowledge and *embrace* our bruises, instead of covering them up or pretending they don't exist, we learn to love better. We become more appreciative, more attentive, and less likely to repeat our past mistakes." My job, then, was to build my future with Jenny, not to replace my past with Beth. By recognizing that both past and present, despair and delight, and heartache and hope could all coexist through the same lens, I could move forward as myself instead of as two irreconcilable versions of me. George empowered me to accept the "whole me"—imperfections, hurts, and all.

Eventually, George and I decided to let Pam and Jenny in on the fun, too. In Jenny's and my regular couples-counseling sessions with George, and our semi-regular dinners with both George and Pam, we explored the joys and challenges of our astonishingly similar early-relationship stories—two reeling, heartbroken men, stuck in an unwanted divorce process; two patient, faithful women in waiting; two wildly improbable encounters, both in time and place; and two redemptive love stories, just at different stages. Over George's famous barbeque ribs and a glass of wine, Pam shared her impressive array of embarrassing gas-station stories (driving off without paying, driving off with the nozzle in her tank, etc.); George shared a variety of embarrassing stories across genres, but mostly focusing on gas of a different variety; I shared my embarrassing cheerleading stories (see Chapter 1); and Jenny blushingly insisted, unconvincingly, that she didn't have any embarrassing stories. Jenny and I treasured George and Pam, not only for their warmth, wisdom, and company, but for the peace they gave us about what our own love could be. With them, it didn't seem like our future was dicey or unclear. It seemed close, God-inspired, and amazing.

* * *

Around this time, our prayers for Amber were increasingly for her spiritual and emotional healing, in addition to her continued physical recuperation. For as Amber's mental cognizance improved and her brain became more alert, she was also more painfully aware of her limitations and the onerous path to recovery. When Amber willed her legs to walk, they hardly budged. When she tried to shout to us, we heard barely-audible whispers. (Dad called these two issues Amber's "walkie-talkie" problems.) Despite Amber's best efforts, her brain's scrambled hardwiring was failing her, and the untangling process was exhausting. She loathed living in a rehabilitation center, apart from her son. And through all of her trials, Amber had not forgotten that she was a young woman. She still wanted to look nice and dress fashionably. She wanted a social life. She wanted to fall in love. But sometimes, the distance between her dreams and her present state just seemed so unbearably vast.

One morning, Amber hoped to attend her friend's wedding shower, but she was thirty minutes late because it took her so long to get ready. My parents (with Bailey) had to pick Amber up and drop her off at the event, like they did when she was a child. When they all returned to

QLI after the shower, Amber was a "basket of emotion," according to my Dad, who wrote the following CaringBridge entry for that day:

It seems that Amber's time with friends today reminded her of the way life was before her accident. She was also down because her walking rehab was not good at all today. Topping that off, she couldn't bear coming back to QLI and watching us leave with Bailey again. When I had a moment to talk alone with her, the two of us had this conversation:

Amber (crying): "Dad, they tell me I'm getting better, but I don't see it. My life is hard for me."

"But you are here, alive, and you are going to get better."

"When? My whole body is broken and I need help with everything. My left side feels like it's asleep all the time. How will I ever marry, and have a wedding shower of my own? How will I ever really live again and do the things Bailey and I used to do together?"

"Your whole body is not broken, honey, and the parts that were have healed well. The Lord also brought you through this without even one surgery—it's amazing. We just need to wait for your brain injury to heal; it's going to take some time. But there's one part of your body that's stronger than it was before. It's your heart, Amber; it's having an impact on people. Many have written us private messages about how this has moved them to Jesus and they believe in prayer once again, or how it has led them to reconcile with a spouse, or talk to a brother or sister for the first time in years. Yes, perhaps 200 stories like this, Amber."

(Still crying) "But why did it have to happen like this? Why so much on me?"

"I don't know, but I do know God sometimes uses his suffering servants to do his greatest work. He's using you, too, Amber."

On Mother's Day, the whole family—Mom, Dad, Amber, Bailey, and me, with Jenny by my side—attended Christ Community Church, my family's longtime church home, at Mom's request on her special day. Amber was just seven years old when we joined Christ Community, but this was her first visit since the accident. Before the service, I reminded Amber of the time when she was ten years old and fell asleep in the middle of the pastor's sermon. Her head, I told Amber, was arched back and plastered to the pew, her eyes rolled, and her mouth gaping, like a deranged zombie. The concerned teenage brother I was, I tried to jolt Amber awake with a swift elbow just below her ribs, which accomplished its intended effect: Amber jerked upward, her back stiffening as if she were electrocuted, as she slurred groggily "I AM AWAKE!" After that embarrassing incident, our poor parents couldn't make eye contact with the pastor for months.

As the Mother's Day service started with songs of praise, the church's worship arts director, Steve Yost, stopped by to welcome us. Quietly, he asked Amber if he could point her out from the altar so members of the large congregation—many of whom had been praying for Amber for the past six months—could see her. Amber nervously agreed. Between songs, Steve excitedly spoke: "Friends, on this Mother's Day, we have a very special mom in attendance. One who has inspired us all for her strength, and who—by the grace of God—is here with us today alongside her own mother, Shelly, and her sweet son, Bailey. Amber, we are so glad you are here—Happy Mother's Day!"

There was a brief, slightly awkward pause as the congregation craned its collective neck in our direction and Amber looked down, self-consciously. Then, some clapping. And then more clapping, which crescendoed into an avalanche of applause, with everyone around us now standing, some teary-eyed, and others tossing in whistling and whoops for good measure. Amber, never the attention-seeker, did not know how to react. Through her own tears of joy, she just whispered: *"I feel so loved."*

*   *   *

As spring blended into summer, and summer into fall, we learned to celebrate Amber's progress in months-long snapshots rather than searching for daily advances and feeling disappointed if they didn't come. Amber navigated around in her wheelchair and practiced walking on QLI's elliptical machines, where she regained muscle memory at her own pace. Eventually, she started using a walker. Soon, she was able to pace down QLI's long hallways if guided by a hip-to-hip helper to walk alongside her and steady her gait. In a development that delighted us all, Amber also became her own biggest fan. One Saturday morning, Jenny and I brought Amber breakfast. Amber, from her wheelchair, told us she first wanted to show us her "new trick." With a smile that could light up Las Vegas, Amber engaged her wheelchair's brakes, scooched to the edge of her seat, and pressed her hands firmly upon on the chair's armrests until she was standing, unassisted. *"Ta-Da!"* Amber exclaimed, hands outstretched. There was nothing small about this accomplishment—she was standing *by herself!*

After she learned to stand, we were all anxious to see Amber take the next step, which would also be her *first step*, unassisted, since the accident. But as the months passed, this feat remained elusive, for reasons as psychological as physiological: Amber was terrified of falling. On CaringBridge, Dad wrote about his efforts to prod Amber into making independent strides:

> After dinner, Amber asked me to stand by as she used each hand to lock its respective brake on her chair. She looked up and smiled, rising on her own. Yes, she has done this before, but the speed in which she did so tonight was excellent. Before, it maybe took her 8-10 seconds to

stand from a sitting position. Tonight, my guess is she did it in 5-6 seconds. A physically well person might do this in 1-2 seconds.

We are getting there.

As she stood at that moment, smiling and triumphant, I took a step or two back and said "Now walk to me."

Well, maybe this was not a great idea on my part, because Amber's smile vanished faster than a physically well person could stand up from a chair, and I could see fear come into her eyes. She froze; couldn't move. I saw her scan the space in front to see what she could hold onto for guidance. Certainly, she wanted to walk—but the confidence was simply gone.

She looked down at the floor, wobbling. I said "I will not let you fall; no way."

Amber looked up: "Can you hold my hand?"

"No." And now I found myself looking into the eyes of beautiful bewilderment.

Seeing that Amber wasn't going to move without a shepherd, I said "You can do this, Amber—I will let your finger wrap around my finger" (trying to show her this is as little as she needed to walk). She took the bait and started moving. Two steps later, Amber buried a renewed smile into my shoulder. I hugged her tight. It was a little muffled, but I heard her thank God.

My goodness, tonight was refreshing. Walking two steps 90% on her own was one thing, but I'm also talking about the return of her happiness, the speedier chair ejection, and the way she prepared a Father's Day card for me.

What a roller coaster week, but I'm thankful of where it stands tonight. And I agree with Amber in thanking God.

More than ever before, Amber began to appreciate the little things in life—which, of course, are often really the biggest things. A karaoke night with Mom; sidewalk-chalk drawing with Bailey at QLI; a standing hug with Dad; volunteering at Seven Salon, where Amber folded towels and interacted with friends. And all along the way, Bailey charmed us with his sweet, comic relief. He seized command over Mom and Dad's nightly prayers, saying, on one occasion, "Dear Jesus, thank you for taking care of Mommy . . . and, and for my friends, and for . . . Play-Doh. Amen." During one drive to QLI, Mom drew Bailey's attention to Creighton Prep, a local all-boys high school. Mom asked Bailey if someday he'd like to go to a boys-only school, or, instead, to a school with both girls and boys. Cleverly, Bailey replied, "I want to go to an all-*girl* school!" In early November, Mom reminded Bailey that his birthday was coming up at the end of the month. "Yes, Gramma, and I will be FOUR!" Bailey answered. Then his pitch rose with excitement as he declared, *"And after that, I will be five and be a MAN, and I will eat my veg-i-dibles!"*

But besides being silly, Bailey also had a special way of touching our hearts. Mom wrote about one such occasion in this CaringBridge journal entry:

Bailey and I dropped Amber off at QLI last night. Bailey looks forward to this every Sunday night since he has his mommy's full attention as Grandma is driving the car. When we left QLI to go back home, he seemed very quiet and was looking out the window from his car seat. A few seconds later he said:

"I see Aunt Kayla up in the sky. She is the brightest and biggest star."

The next thing he said was:

"Grandma, I have a question for you."

When he starts sentences like that, I always have to be prepared for whatever comes next. His question was:

"If Kayla had an accident and mommy had an accident, then why is Kayla in Heaven and mommy is here?"

I said:

"God really needed Kayla in Heaven to help him, but God knew how much you needed your mommy here on earth to take care of you."

"Oh."

Bailey sees and accepts everything, simply and clearly. He lets the hardest things for most people to deal with just bounce off of him. It's no wonder Jesus loves the little children.

*　*　*

As another Thanksgiving rolled closer, my life was bursting with reminders of how much my family and I had to be thankful for. By then, Amber had shuffled her feet, by herself, five times ever-so-slightly forward, but we called it "walking" nonetheless. Dad described the moment as, "One small step for man; five small steps for womankind!"

Brimming with confidence, Amber ramped up her therapy regimen and set bigger goals for herself. By November 5, 2011—one year since the date of her accident—Amber could take more than a dozen steps by herself, ambling halfway across a room unassisted. And her ambition and self-esteem were soaring.

In the eight-month span after I moved back to Omaha, my love for Jenny grew exponentially. She was my gift from God, and I woke up every morning vowing to treat her so. Over time, I learned more and more how perfectly we complimented each other—like two unique puzzle pieces snapping crisply together, matching one's strengths to the other's weaknesses to make a seamless whole. I helped Jenny realize her inner fortitude, voice, and leadership, challenging her to see the great things she could do—and that *God* could do *through* her—when she stepped out of her comfort zone. Jenny helped me experience a purer faith, one less defined by ritual and more defined by a heart that seeks God. Her patience, love, and steady nature helped restore my scared, wounded spirit. During one of our counseling sessions with Pastor George, he stared at us and beamed, joyfully exclaiming, "Isn't this great?! Isn't God so good?!" Shaking his head and still smiling, George went on, "If you ever need a reminder about what God's love looks like, just look at each other." As George explained it, God didn't *need* to do anything to help Jenny and me, or to bring us together—God's love was already made perfect when he sent his Son to redeem and restore us. George called Jenny's and my relationship "grace heaped on grace." A reflection of a love that is unconditional and overflows, and which has nothing to do with what we deserve and everything to do with God's abundant goodness. We viewed our relationship as a living reminder of God's rich generosity, as captured in Ephesians 2:8-9: "For it is by *grace* you have been saved, through faith—and *this is not from yourselves, it is the gift of God*—not by works, so that no one can boast."

At the church's request, I agreed to speak at West Hills' Thanksgiving Eve service. I shared my journey—basically, the abridged version of this book. But most importantly, I gave God a lot of much-deserved thanks and praise.

I thanked God for Pastor Phil and Ravenswood Covenant Church in Chicago, whose members performed spiritual CPR on me during the past year's crises. They fed me; they shared a beer with me; they played basketball with me; they let me stay in their homes during the awful, lonely stretch between Thanksgiving and Christmas; they cared for my dogs, and later adopted them when I moved back to Omaha.

I thanked God for my new West Hills family, who had so warmly welcomed me during my transition home. I thanked God for George, whose words had steadied me, and whose guidance kept my path straight when life's trials threatened to overpower my ability to cope with them. George helped me believe that a ship anchored by God will not capsize; the crashing waves will not overwhelm it.

I thanked God for so many friends, whose love I had never fully seen until they cared for me in crisis. For my closest friends, who opened their homes to me, who prayed ceaselessly with me, who supported me as I asked God for a miraculous reconciliation with Beth, and who helped me pick up the pieces when none came. For a new friend, who popped into my life seemingly out of nowhere and coached me through my despair in daily texts and phone calls where she promised me, again and again, that my life would not always stink, and that she would keep repeating this promise until I believed it. (And she did.)

I thanked God for my family. For my Dad, whose love and sacrifice for his wife and children is boundless. He alone has clawed through the many legal and financial complexities of Amber's ongoing medical care and support needs, and it was at his urging that I finally decided to write this book, after months of hesitation and deliberation. For my Mom, who devoted her entire adult life to raising my siblings and me, and who has doubled down on her commitment by offering the same selfless care, again, to both Amber and Bailey as their primary caregivers.

For Amber, who has battled through more in her young life than anyone I know but has come through it stronger, not weaker. She inspires and amazes me. And for Bailey, my resilient nephew, who teaches us so much about life, even as we do our best to teach him a thing or two, too.

I thanked God for Jenny—my "grace heaped on grace"—who God used to resuscitate my heart and give my life meaning again. The term "girlfriend," I told the West Hills crowd, could never do justice to what Jenny's love had done for me.

And I praised God for his pure, overpowering mercy. I never would have wished suffering on myself, or on my family. But when it came, God used it to draw us closer to him—and isn't that what's most important? I had never before experienced God's love as deeply as I did during these trials. That God also saw fit to go the extra step to restore me and bless me with Jenny was almost more than I could comprehend.

Several times during my Thanksgiving Eve talk, my eyes drifted to my family and Jenny, who were seated together and shedding a few joyful tears along with me. *Yes*, I thought—*this Thanksgiving, we all have so much to be thankful for*.

* * *

It was the Friday after Thanksgiving, and Jenny and I were decorating her Christmas tree. Exactly one year ago that day, Jenny and I had traded our first words on Facebook when she responded to my Thanksgiving Day note. To commemorate the anniversary, I crafted (with significant help from my artsy secretary) a series of ornaments detailing important milestones in our journey together. There was our first meal together—(drum roll, please) Arby's, when Jenny and I visited Amber together in Lincoln—memorialized by an ornamental carton of twisted brown pipe cleaners that vaguely resembled curly-cue fries. There was a mini FedEx truck with a wreath on the back, which paid homage to one of Jenny's early Facebook-message quips, when she shared her belief that if we return our broken hearts to God, he will honor their "manufacturer's warranty" by fixing them and sending them back to us when we are ready to love again. There was an ornament capturing our first Nebraska football game together—a rain-soaked rally from a 21-point second-half deficit against Ohio State, the greatest comeback win in Husker history. And a handful of others—ornaments remembering the first flowers I gave Jenny, a bouquet of Gerbera daisies; our first date; and the Facebook exchange when Jenny told me she "kind of felt the same way" about our future together.

The final ornament was a dazzling, decorative miniature carriage adorned with the most important delivery of the day, which would not arrive via FedEx: Jenny's sparkling, custom-made engagement ring. "Jenny, falling in love with you this past year, after I thought I'd lost everything, has helped me to better understand God's perfect love for me. I am so happy I found you waiting for me on the other side of the dark cloud. You are the greatest gift I've ever received, and I want to treasure that gift for the rest of our lives. Will you marry me?" Jenny pounced on me with an onslaught of squeals, hugs, and kisses. And somewhere in that commotion, I got the answer I was looking for: "YES!!!"

CHAPTER 11

"And over all these virtues put on love, which binds them all together in perfect unity."

—COLOSSIANS 3:14

On a perfect spring afternoon in Temecula, California, I stood outdoors with Pastor George underneath a vaulted, vine-wrapped arbor at the end of a cobblestone walkway, waiting for my bride. Amidst the blue-sky backdrop under wispy cloud traces haloed by the sun, and with rolling, vineyard-peppered foothills unfolding behind us, it was easy to sense that God was near. "The whole day felt like a prayer," Jenny later said of our wedding day. "A single, extended prayer of thankfulness." With us were thirty of our closest friends and family members who knew our journeys and how much this day meant to us.

Including Amber. Jenny and I often called Amber "our little cupid" because of how God used her recovery to pen the first sentences of our love story. Amber eagerly accepted her title, kiddingly reminding us at every opportunity that we "owed" her "big time." Two months before our wedding, Amber was released from QLI to my parents' home, where she could live with Bailey as she continued her recovery through outpatient rehabilitation therapy. After 450 days spent in three facilities—20 days at the Med Center, 92 days at Madonna, and 338 days at QLI—Amber was finally under the same roof as her son, which was all she needed to call it "home." And now—in a development that once might have seemed too incredible to be true—Amber was in California, celebrating with us. As my sister slowly walked with Dad down the courtyard's center aisle to her first-row seat, she beamed at me through proud, happy tears that streaked down her cheeks from behind her sunglasses.

Jenny emerged from the bridal cottage on her father's arm to our harpist's rendition of Canon in D, her blissful gaze fixed squarely on me with every nearing step.   Joyful flashes of my road to Jenny flooded over me, each image captioned by a single prayer: *Thank you, God.* I owed him. Big time. A lifetime of Jenny's love and companionship felt like a treasure of inestimable value, a gift I did not deserve and surely could never repay. In that moment, I saw our union as a microcosm of God's very nature—his infinite, unconditional, *saving* love, which my limited understanding could never fully unpack—distilled to a still-overwhelming "condensed version" in this tangible form. I cannot wrap my head around God's timeless, boundless goodness and grace, but I can hold onto Jenny, reflect on the highs and lows of my journey, and begin to taste the essence of the redemption God freely offers.

As Jenny got closer, she smiled giddily at me and her gait picked up a tick, her eyes welling with moisture and her curly locks bobbing in the breeze. Her father handed her off to me, and she and I held hands, rejoining George for the scripture readings and exchanging of our vows. I went first:

Jenny,

I've spent a lot of time lately searching for words that do justice to the way I feel about you. Unfortunately, time and again, words have failed me. Which is a huge bummer, because saying what I think is one of my few strengths!

"I love you" seems like a good starting place. But I also love the Huskers, and burritos, so we can't just stop there.

I've tried mixing in adverbs, but those haven't worked either. "I love you *very* much." "I love you *so* much." Or even stringing them together: "I love you *so* *very* much!" These words still seem so inadequate in describing how I feel.

My sweet Jenny, I wish I could tell you. I wish I had the words. How can I possibly explain this journey?

Just 18 months ago, I thought I could never love or be loved again. Then I saw a photo of you. As I've told you often, when I first saw you I thought you were the most beautiful woman I had ever seen. That is more true today than ever. And just at the sight of you, I felt . . . hope. It was a hope completely unhinged from reality, though . . . . The way one "hopes" to win the lottery, or the way a little boy "hopes" he grows up to be a super hero. A sweet thought, but not real.

So maybe you can imagine my excitement when, seemingly out of nowhere, you just said hello to me. And then we became pen pals. And then friends. And now we're standing here today, at the altar, committing the rest of our lives to each other. The feeling is indescribable. Words fail me.

The counterpart to my love for you is my thankfulness to God. For putting friends, family, and mentors in my life who could hold me up . . . sometimes *physically* hold me up . . . and who helped rebuild me to love you. I'm thankful to God for nudging me to become Facebook friends with you for some reason five years ago even though we didn't know each other. I'm thankful you accepted! I'm thankful that God healed my sister, and that he used her recovery as a platform for introducing us.

And I'm also thankful for the hardships that I had to endure to get to you. The word "light" means nothing unless we have experienced the contrast of darkness. In the same way, I could not have fully appreciated the gift of your love without first feeling the depths of hopelessness. I don't know how or why God interacts with us. But I know he created you, in part, to be my life preserver, and a solid anchor to build a family upon as we move forward together.

At this point, I've said a lot for a guy who opened by saying words couldn't explain how I feel. So I'll close with one final observation: although actions really do speak louder than words, they, too, will never fully capture my devotion to you. No amount of opening your car door, or rubbing your feet, or cooking you breakfast will ever get me to the point where I will lean back and say "OK, that should do it." My actions, like my words, will never be enough.

But that doesn't mean I won't try. Instead, I'll happily spend the rest of my life telling you and showing you how deeply I adore you, knowing full well that I'll never quite get there. My only hope is that in the end, you'll have finally begun to get a small sense of what I mean when I say "I love you."

As I tucked away my vows, Jenny unfolded hers, reading them aloud to me:

I stand here feeling overwhelmed by God's grace. I cannot thank him or praise him enough for the gift of your heart. He is the author of our love story. He used our past joys and trials to prepare us for one another. He used those trials to refine us and deepen our trust in him. Following his whispers was what brought me to you. Our love is my reminder that if I seek and trust God's will, he will not only protect and strengthen me, but bless me abundantly for this faith. Second Corinthians 4:17 says: "Our light and momentary troubles are achieving for us an eternal glory that far outweighs them all." I feel God has given me a glimpse of this in you.

The love I feel for you comes from the deepest part of my heart. It is the part of my heart that is completely still. It is the part of my heart where God meets me. It is the type of love God taught me how to freely offer and receive. This love is pure, unconditional, and selfless. I am blessed to share my journey with a man who encourages and strengthens me, treasures and respects me, and loves me as I am while pointing me towards the Lord for growth. Your affection, loyalty, thoughtfulness, strength, sense of humor, and faith bring me so much happiness. My soul feels simultaneously at peace and overjoyed when I am beside you.

I will continue to seek God's guidance as I commit to the role of your wife. I know our Lord will continue to lead us and strengthen us on this journey. I promise to cherish you, encourage you, and stand by you for the rest of my life. You are the man God perfectly and uniquely designed for me to walk through life with.

With Jenny's sweet words still echoing through the depths of my consciousness, George walked us through our "I do"s, where Jenny and I promised to love each other for the rest of our lives. Then, George led us in a prayer written by Dr. Louis Evans. It was the same one that George and Pam prayed on their wedding day:

God of love, you have established marriage for the happiness and welfare of humankind. Yours was the plan and only with you can we work it out with joy. As we join together in marriage, our joys are doubled, since the happiness of one is the happiness of the other. Our burdens are halved; when we share them, we divide the load.

Bless Ryan; may his strength and gentleness be Jenny's boast and pride. May he live so that she finds in him the honor that the heart of a woman deserves.

Bless Jenny; give her a tenderness that will make her great; a deep sense of understanding and a great faith in you.

Teach them both that marriage is not merely for themselves. It is two uniting and joining hands to serve you. May they seek the kingdom of God and your righteousness, and all other things shall be added unto them. May they not expect perfection of each other—that belongs only to you—but may they see each other through a lover's kind and patient eyes.

Now make such assignments to them on the scroll of your will as will bless them and develop their character. Give them only enough tears to keep them tender, only enough hurts to keep them humane, only enough failure to keep their hands tightly clinched in yours, and enough success to make them sure that they walk with their God. May they never take each other's love for granted, but experience that breathless wonder that exclaims, "Out of the whole world, you have chosen me!"

When life is done and the sun is setting, may they be found then as now, side by side, still thanking God for each other. May they serve you faithfully and happily together until at last one day, one lays the other in the arms of God.

This we ask through Jesus Christ, the great lover of our souls.

Toward the end of the prayer, a rabbit danced onto our pathway, pausing briefly to perch between Jenny and me and pose for the photographer. My parents—who believe God sometimes uses nature to remind us of lost loved ones—were delighted, thinking immediately of our family's biggest animal lover, Kayla. The rabbit darted away on George's "amen." Finally, George presented Jenny and me to the crowd and instructed me to kiss my bride—a command I dutifully heeded. We exited, side-by-side, hands locked, joyfully accepting the gift God gave us and marching onward toward the next leg of our journey—*together*.

CHAPTER 12

"The goal of redemption is not immediate happiness as we might define it now, but holiness of life; not the good life as we imagine it here on earth, but the perfection of heaven itself—a completion, enlargement, and perfection of what we experience in this life."
—JERRY SITTSER, *A GRACE REVEALED*

After our wedding, Jenny and I honeymooned in Hawaii. I packed everything I needed into a single duffel bag. For most of the trip, Jenny wore casual tees, shorts, swimsuits, and flip-flops—no matter, she still somehow managed to cram a monster-sized suitcase and two carry-ons with what I could only assume were cast-iron anvils, which I laboriously lugged around the islands while Jenny sipped Mai Tais. As we settled into married life after our honeymoon, we committed to praying together nightly. For months, Jenny called me to "tuck her in" at night by reading my vows to her; like a little girl nodding off to a Cinderella story, Jenny fell asleep with a soft smile. Time has not diluted my thankfulness for God's heaping grace or the gift of Jenny, and I don't suspect it ever will. Every night as my head hits the pillow beside her, I think I couldn't possibly love Jenny any more. But each morning, I wake up to find my love for her has grown.

My parents recently built a ranch-style home that allows them to reside on the main floor while Amber and Bailey live with some autonomy on the basement level. Mom and Dad have experienced God's redemptive grace most tangibly through Amber's healing, Bailey's sweet heart and resiliency, and the community's outpouring of support—both in Omaha and beyond. Meanwhile, Amber's physical limitations have only multiplied her spiritual yearning. More than ever before, she thanks God for her blessings—especially a life spent watching her son grow—and praises him for every "baby step" in her recovery.

Things are neither easy nor perfect. God never promised they would be. Amber still struggles tremendously to perform the basic functions that most of us take for granted, like walking, living independently, and speaking at a conversational volume and tempo. Her medical bills have already neared the dump-truck driver's insurance limits, her therapy needs are ongoing, and, despite her best efforts, she may never work again. For my part, my wounded past makes me fret and fixate more than I probably should about death and about losing Jenny in some sudden and unexpected way. Sometimes, I feel like I'm holding my breath in anticipation for the next unforeseen and crushing disappointment, which might come at any time. I still feel sad, baffled, and somewhat scared when I think about how things fell apart with Beth. Like everyone else in my family, I still miss Kayla dearly and think about her almost every day.

But we have learned to thank God for our blessings and to keep praising him through our trials—a virtue that was marvelously and inspirationally reinforced to me in the past year by my friend and mentor, Pastor George. In December 2002, about ten years before I met him, George saw a doctor for a routine physical and learned he had Waldenstrom's lymphoma: a rare, slow-growing, treatable, but incurable cancer. George underwent an immune-system-boosting treatment with excruciating side effects, and afterward, doctors told him he had five to seven years to live. Three years later, George found a lump on the side of his face. It was a clear-cell tumor on his parotid gland, and doctors likely could not remove it without taking George's jaw—and his preaching career—with it. While doctors operated on George, Pam wept and prayed in the hospital chapel, begging God to save her husband and to spare his capacity to preach. Incredibly, doctors removed the tumor and salvaged George's jaw. George needed reconstructive surgery and months' worth of preventative radiation, but he never stopped preaching.

What followed were five years of healthy, vibrant, God-blessed remission. George took up jogging—four miles every day—and vacationed yearly with Pam to Colorado, where he woke up early each morning, coffee mug in hand, to watch the sun peek over the horizon, warming his flesh and draping the mountains in light. Once, George uploaded the majestic scene onto his Facebook profile, exclaiming "This is what heaven looks like!" During his remission, George took numerous mission trips to China, dug fresh-water wells in Africa, and enriched thousands of lives—mine included—with his wisdom, companionship, and spirit-filled sermons. God used George to help heal me from my divorce and to prepare me to love Jenny; his counsel helped pour the faith-filled foundation that would eventually become the bedrock of our marriage.

On August 21, 2011, George preached a sermon titled "Into Deep Water," which he prefaced by telling the congregation that "this message was birthed from more deeply within my soul than any other in my 17 years of preaching." The sermon's text was Luke 5:1-11, where Jesus tells Peter (then a fisherman) to draw his boat into "deep water" and "let down the nets for a catch." Peter resists, saying "Master, we've worked hard all night and haven't caught anything." But he also complies: "Because you say so, I will let down the nets." Jesus' command wasn't comfortable—the fishermen had labored all evening, tiring fruitlessly, when Jesus told them to start over and try again. Nor was it logical, at least by their standards—the prime fishing time had passed, and typically, shallow water, not deep water, was the better bet for a hefty catch. But as soon as they obeyed Jesus' call, their nets became flush with fish— so many that they had to signal another boat to help them bring in the haul, with both boats starting to sink under the catch's massive weight. Amazed, Peter fell at Jesus' feet, proclaiming him Lord. "Do not be afraid," Jesus replied, calling Peter into discipleship—"from now on you will fish for people."

George closed his Bible and told us God was laying three heavy messages on his heart. First, "the spiritual life of the church of America has become anemic." In John 16:33, Jesus says "take heart!" for "I have overcome the world." But is this true today—or has the world overcome the church? As Christians, we are called to *transform* the world, not to conform to it. (Romans 12:2) By diluting our "Christ-distinctiveness" and politicizing our mission, George feared the light of the church was dimming in the darkness of the world. "Only when the light of Jesus Christ shines in the church of America," George said, "will the net fill with fish."

Second, God is calling each of us to deeper water in our spiritual journeys. The fishermen in Luke 5 didn't want to cast another net after a long night of work, but they did it because Jesus told them to. Elsewhere in the gospel (Matthew 14), Jesus walks on water and invites Peter to join him, saying only "Come." With that one word, Peter trades his boat's secure footing for the gusty winds and crashing waves of a predawn storm. "Jesus' call will always pull us out of the pews and into the water," George said. Jesus' call may require us to leave the shallow end, where we wade, and to enter the deep end, where we swim, thrash, and gasp for God—like Peter did when his fleeting faith sunk him just before Jesus clutched his hand and pulled him up to safety.

Third, *there is an urgency in this call*." "This is the hardest point for me to articulate," George confessed. "But I am very clear that God is telling me there is a window of opportunity for us that is narrowing." In several places, the Bible references a "lampstand"—a traditional Jewish symbol for God's presence that Jesus assumed when he declared "I am the light of the world." (John 8:12) God handed us the lampstand, but he can also "remove" it at his will. (Revelations 2:4-5) George feared the church was losing its grip on the lampstand, and only by heeding Jesus' deep-water call could we keep it. "I believe that each of us will be required to take the next step in our journey," George said. For every person, the journey will look different. But "the places where we have heard the Lord call, but we have decided not to go . . . those are the places God is asking us to go." Wrapping up, George said:

> This is a call I can no longer ignore. It is a call that I feel such a deep conviction to. We are to step up our life of discipleship by moving into deeper water. I believe it is what Jesus Christ is asking you and I to do. And I hope you will join me in this journey. Amen.

* * *

Little did George know that the words he spoke—the urgency of the call, the narrowing of the window, and the extinguishing of the light; concepts George felt God planted in the very core of his being— would take on such deeply personal meanings in the year ahead. The day before our wedding in Temecula, Jenny and I took George and Pam to our venue to walk through the ceremony and, more importantly, to enjoy some wine-tasting. Amidst stories and laughter that echoed across the vineyard's valleys, Jenny and I were struck, again, by how thankful we were for George and Pam's friendship and the model of their marriage.

In the following month, though, George began to feel unusually winded and fatigued. His six-month lymphoma checkup revealed falling red blood-cell counts—a concerning development that would require further testing. On May 27, 2012—one day before George's follow-up cancer screening—Pam was reading from the book *One Thousand Gifts* by Ann Voskamp and reflecting on the nature of grace. Pam realized that during the past five years—while she and George lived happy, healthy lives, far exceeding George's initial prognosis in 2002—it had been easy to receive God's grace, and to praise him. But what would happen if God's grace got messy? In her book, Voskamp writes extensively about the Greek word *eucharisteo*, which roughly translates to "thanksgiving." But *eucharisteo* is not just a word reserved for cheery times. In fact, it's the very word the New Testament uses to capture Jesus' prayer to God during the Last Supper—in the same breath that Jesus predicted his imminent betrayal and death. (Matthew 26:20-29) *Eucharisteo* embodies the kind of praise Job gave God after he lost his children, his pride, and everything he owned, still proclaiming: "The Lord gave, and the Lord has taken away; *blessed be the name of the Lord.*" (Job 1:21) The Bible asks us to "*always* give thanks to God for *everything*" (Eph. 5:20)—not only to thank God for our most apparent blessings. When we recognize this, Voskamp writes, we see that *all is grace*; God is *always good* and we are *always loved*; and *everything is eucharisteo*—deserving of our thanks. Just as a surgeon may cut into the body to clean out disease, says

Voskamp, God may use painful life events to cut into our wayward hearts: to transfigure and elevate them; to make us more like him; to make us whole and allow true healing to begin.

Pam's personal journal entry from May 29, two days later, summarizes what happened next:

> Yesterday we went to see Dr. Armitage and learned that George's lymphoma is back. He will start treatment on June 20th. The news was so hard. But Lord, you prepared me when I was reading *One Thousand Gifts* the other night, and I considered the question: "What if the news isn't good—what of grace, then?" I felt the whole chapter speaking to my heart, and as I read it I knew that You were preparing me . . . I knew in my heart that this is where You were taking us.
>
> I laid awake last night . . . not worrying or fretting, but pondering. I drifted in and out, but at one point I was awakened and I felt like your Spirit spoke to my heart saying "Cancer, the Grace Teacher is back." I thought about how we have a choice about how we respond to this disease. I thought about how I pray and hope and want George to be healed, but if this doesn't end the way we want it to . . . you will still be enough, and your grace will still be there. It really is a matter of perspective.
>
> This quote from *One Thousand Gifts* touched me, and I have returned to it again and again: "The quiet song of gratitude, *eucharisteo*, lures humility out of the shadows because to receive a gift the knee must bend humble and the hand must lie vulnerably open and *the will must bow to accept whatever the Giver chooses to give.*"

And so George and Pam made their decision: they would praise God, hands open, ready to receive his grace in whatever form he chose to give it. George openly lobbied God for fifteen more years of health—an audacious request he knew only God could grant. George kept up his jogging regimen throughout June and July, knowing good health was imperative for his body's response to the resumed lymphoma-suppression treatment. But on August 16, George returned from his run complaining of back pain. He'd felt soreness there for weeks, but now the pain was sharper and more severe. At Pam's insistence, they returned to the hospital for an MRI. When the scanned images of George's upper body came back, they were almost too difficult to take in: a white, webby spattering of new masses invading George's lungs, ribs, and spine—the source of George's back pain. Further testing would confirm that George's clear-cell carcinoma—the condition that plagued his jaw in 2005—was back, reuniting with his lymphoma. The clear-cell carcinoma had metastasized, and it was now a Stage IV cancer—the final stage. To survive, George would need a miracle.

George was seemingly unfazed. In an email to friends and family, George celebrated the positives, noting that the cancer on his spine was putting so much pressure on his nervous system that his doctors couldn't understand why he wasn't already experiencing paralysis. "We know it is God's faithfulness!" George explained. He also reiterated his prayer for fifteen more years of healthy living, clarifying that "More would be good! I'm just trying not to be greedy . . . " In an email, George shared the following passage from Daniel 3:16-18, which he described as his and Pam's "statement" during his cancer battle:

> Shadrach, Meshach and Abednego replied to him, "King Nebuchadnezzar, we do not need to defend ourselves before you in this matter. If we are thrown into the blazing furnace, the God we serve is able to deliver us from it, and he will deliver us from Your Majesty's hand. But even if he does not, we want you to know, Your Majesty, that we will not

serve your gods or worship the image of gold you have set up."

George knew God could deliver him from the "blazing furnace" of Stage IV cancer, just as he had delivered his trusting servants from the fire in Daniel 3. *But even if he didn't*, God was still God, and George would continue to praise him. "We believe God will prove faithful," George wrote. "And no matter what, we choose to trust him! We will not bend a knee to fear or doubt!"

Incredibly, George continued to preach. "I will begin radiation tomorrow and be at work Friday," George wrote in an email update. One year earlier, George's sermon series had encouraged listeners to journey *into* deeper water in our walks with God. Now, George increasingly found solace in the idea of God rescuing him from those harsh waters and calling him home. George quoted 2 Samuel 22:17-20:

> He reached down from on high and took hold of me;
> He *drew me out of deep waters.*
> He rescued me from my powerful enemy,
> from my foes, who were too strong for me.
> They confronted me in the day of my disaster,
> but the Lord was my support.
> He brought me out into a spacious place.

*   *   *

I wrote the first half of this book with a very heavy heart—not only because of the painful memories and emotions the writing process stirred, but because another key character in my life, someone I loved and who had given so much to me, was suffering. I shared every chapter with George as I wrote it. Every time, he wrote or called me back with the encouragement I needed to start the next difficult chapter.

I wanted George to live long enough to read the whole book. I didn't want this book's final chapters to also be George's. But as the weeks passed, it seemed he and I were both losing a race against time.

In mid-September, George's children flew in for the weekend from Texas, Maryland, and Colorado to celebrate his 63rd birthday a few months early. It was a happy reunion calendared long in advance. As it turned out, it would also be the last weekend George walked. In the following weeks, George pressed onward through his sermon series as the tumor on his vertebrae slowly squeezed its grip on his spine like a vice, cinching off George's lower-body functioning. In consecutive weeks, George preached standing independently; then with a cane; and then from a wheelchair. After his decade-long battle with lymphoma, multiple bouts of clear-cell cancer, a grueling schedule of radiation and other therapies, and new skin cancers popping up on George's tissue, it seemed George was finally breaking down under cancer's full-body assault.

Still, he preached. Until October 21, when George delivered what would be, unbeknownst to him, his final sermon. Its title: "Costly Discipleship." The text was Luke 14:25-35, a difficult passage where Jesus warns that "whoever does not carry their cross and follow me cannot be my disciple." George looked down, and his voice softened. "I thought, this week, as I sat in this chair and my legs grew weaker ... that if this is the cross I bear, then this is the cross I bear." George explained: "I think sometimes we spend so much time praying our way *out* of the cross. What we should be doing is praying our way *through* the cross." The point of our lives, George said, is not to experience the abundance of pleasure or the absence of pain. It's not to live a little longer or even to feel a little happier. "It's *total submission to the cross*. That's the bottom line of discipleship—to die unto ourselves; to nail our desires to the cross, and carry it for Christ." George's voice strengthened with conviction as he continued:

> The cross changes every relationship. When we die to ourselves, our marriage changes. When we die to ourselves, we make different choices about our jobs. When we die to

ourselves, we make different choices about lifestyle. When we die to ourselves, we're able to serve the kingdom of God in new ways. We have a different social life, a different prayer life, a different way of seeing the world ... Carrying the cross means dying to ourselves, but it is the only path to knowing joy and mercy and God's love.

With his knee bowed and his hands open, George had prayed for a miracle while accepting the cross. And in his final sermon, he encouraged us all to do the same. George finished with a prayer that he wove into Galatians 2:20, the last verse he would recite as our pastor: "I have been crucified with Christ, and *I no longer live.*" George's voice cracked as he could not fight the tears. *"But Christ lives in me. The life I live in this body, I live by faith in the Son of God, who loves me and gave his life for me. Amen."*

Four days later, George suffered a perforated bowel and required surgery—a drastic operation made even more dangerous because George's system was by then brimming with blood thinners. "No fear," George messaged me as he prepared to enter the operating room. "The Lord is in this!" Twenty-two stitches later, George survived his surgery. But soon thereafter, George and his family made an important decision. "My choice is no more chemo," George wrote in an email update to friends. "With this decision, I will most likely not leave here (the hospital) to go home. I will likely go to hospice. There's no telling when that might happen—in days, weeks, or longer." "This is not easy, but we are at peace with this," George said. "I am still working on living, which from our perspective we do in every moment, even as we try to be ready when the Lord calls." "How much I love each of you, and am so thankful for all of you! So, we will just keep making this journey. Bless each of you!"

When I read George's email, I felt engulfed with sadness and fear that I may never see him again. I immediately replied:

George, I have to be honest: Jenny's and my hearts broke for you when we read this update. For a while, we just held each other and cried. I just met you two years ago, and now it is very hard and very sad for me to consider a world where you aren't walking along with me, as my friend and mentor.

When I lost Kayla, I always wished I could have had just one last conversation with her before she was gone. A conversation where I could say all of the things I never made a point to say before, because I always thought she'd be with me. A conversation that I could fondly reflect on to get me through the sad days until I saw her again—however or whenever that might be. But now, here I am with you— one of the most important people God has placed in my life, who I've watched battle cancer for months. And I still feel like I've done and said so little to show you how much I care for you, and how thankful I am that God brought you into my life.

George, *thank you.* Thank you for loving me; thank you for allowing God's perfect love to shine through you; thank you for teaching me; thank you for being my friend. You are precious to me.

Your friend and brother in Christ,

Ryan

Within minutes, George answered: "We love you so much! Ryan, God is so faithful! He will walk with you! We have time to talk more! So hold together! I love you both so much and believe in you!" And sure enough, God allowed Jenny and me several more precious visits with George. On each occasion, we struggled to toe the line between maintaining a sense of positive normalcy and saying the things we wanted to say if this meeting was our last. On one visit, I failed miserably, sobbing and telling George I didn't want to lose him. He set down his fork between his sandwich and a bunch of grapes, and then picked up his Bible. (Despite his condition, George maintained his appetite until the end.) He read aloud a scriptural passage written by the Apostle Paul, from prison, that George said captured perfectly his sentiment on living and dying.

Philippians 1:18-27:

Yes, and I will continue to rejoice, for I know that through your prayers and God's provision of the Spirit of Jesus Christ what has happened to me will turn out for my deliverance. I eagerly expect and hope that I will in no way be ashamed, but will have sufficient courage so that now as always *Christ will be exalted in my body, whether by life or by death. For to me, to live is Christ and to die is gain.* If I am to go on living in the body, this will mean fruitful labor for me. Yet what shall I choose? I do not know! I am torn between the two: *I desire to depart and be with Christ,* which is better by far; but it is more necessary for you that I remain in the body. Convinced of this, I know that I will remain, and I will continue with all of you for your progress and joy in the faith, so that through my being with you again your boasting in Christ Jesus will abound on account of me.

Then George closed his Bible and looked at me as I wiped away tears. "Ryan, you've already experienced so much loss in your life. It's given you this deep reservoir of pain, and losing me will probably tap into that and resurface a lot of sad feelings. But you need to know something—this is not a tragedy." George's eyes were wide and intense, underscoring his adamancy on this point: *"This is not a tragedy!* This is not sudden. I've lived a great life! God's already helped me beat cancer—twice!" "We are all going to die someday," George continued.

146

"When I die, I know *exactly* where I'm going! You see this as me being torn away from Pam, torn away from you, torn away from life," George said. "But it's not like that at all. I'm not being torn away from anything; I'm being *carried to Jesus*." George reminded me: "We're all called to carry the cross and to submit to God's will. My cross is cancer. *But the cross is not just death—it's resurrection! It's life! It's salvation!*" I held George's hand, trying to wrap my head around his words. Then, after a long pause, George flipped a switch in the way only he could, raising one eyebrow, pointing his fork at me, and asking with a smirk: "Wanna grape?"

In George's typical selfless fashion, he seemed less concerned about death than about others' reactions to it. In one conversation and in text messages, George reminded Jenny that his passing would be hard on me and asked her to "take care of Ryan's heart" when he was gone. In early November, my Mom emailed George to thank him for all he had done for me. George replied: "I have done very little! You have a wonderful son. I'm sorry my journey is adding to his pain, but hopefully he is seeing something profound being modeled by Jesus! That's my prayer . . . Bless you! - George."

George and Pam made gratitude a habit, thanking God at the start and end of every day "for his countless blessings in our lives," Pam later told me. "Each night before I left the Rehab Center," Pam said, "George would look at me and say 'it was a good day today.'" And of course, George continued his ministry through his last days, converting his hospital room into his office. When a group of George's closest friends visited him to lay hands on him and pray, he inspired them all when, through tears, George thanked God for his cancer—the "Grace Teacher." "Thank you for the cross," George cried. "Thank you for dying for me! Thank you for using this disease to draw me closer and make me more like you in suffering. *Thank you for the journey!*" Through everything, George almost had us all convinced he was lucky for his affliction. In the days leading up to November 16, George's birthday, hundreds of cards from all around the world flooded his room with words of thanks, love, and celebration. When Jenny and I visited him, George gleefully told us about cards he'd received from old friends and showed us a photo of Chinese peasants sitting in a circle and praying for him. George choked up, his eyes welling: "Peasants in China are praying for *me!* What did I ever do to deserve this? This is one of the neatest things that's ever happened in my life!" George looked around the room—at Pam, at Jenny, at me. "Who *gets* this?" I told George I didn't understand. *"This!"* George exclaimed. "This moment! This life! Here and now! I am so *blessed!* I feel amazing! I mean, I can't move my legs—but other than that, I feel great!" As death approached, George grasped more than ever the gift of each breath—his love for life was amazing and contagious.

Days later, West Hills Church hosted Bob Goff, author of the book *Love Does*, to lead a special worship service. In addition to writing a New York Times bestseller, Bob is a skilled attorney and the founder of Restore International, a nonprofit human rights organization with a simple mission: fight injustice, wherever it may be found. Bob's love for the Lord is infectious and effusive. I've never met anyone remotely like him. The core of Bob's message is that God is downright giddy in love with us. Imagine God and all of heaven eagerly gathered around a balcony, anxiously gazing below to catch a glimpse of what wonderful things you will do next. That's the God Bob knows and loves. Bob's friends like to say he "leaks Jesus" because Christ's joy seems to seep right through him, compelling him to *act* out love—whimsically, unconventionally, and extravagantly—not just talk about it. Bob enjoys a good "caper"— an impromptu escapade where God's love alone guides adventure and outreach. Before Bob's visit, George strongly encouraged Jenny and me to join Bob for a caper somewhere exotic. "This is the opportunity of a lifetime!" George insisted.

Bob's capers have taken him thousands of miles at the drop of a hat. But on this trip, Jenny, I, and another young couple from West Hills would join Bob for a caper just a few miles west on Dodge Street, where Pam had planned a surprise get-together with George on a Sunday afternoon after church. When George saw us, his grin lit up the room. Bob walked in, removed his shoes, and encouraged us to do the same, because "we're standing on holy ground." Bob explained: "George, we can hardly even see you any more—we see *straight through you to Jesus*." As George's physical body withered, his frailty revealed Christ's image; it seemed we were all witnessing the transformation Paul wrote about in Galatians 2:20, the verse George closed with in his final sermon: "*I have been crucified with Christ and I no longer live, but Christ lives in me.*" Bob rubbed his hand on George's head, which was now bare from the past months' chemotherapy, and together we all prayed. Pam thanked God for teaching her about the nature of grace through George's trials, and for the opportunity to journey through life with her loving husband. A few others also prayed, and then the room fell still for a moment. Then, to my astonishment, Jenny chimed in, praying out loud for the first time in her life. Jenny thanked God for putting a message on George's heart to call us all to deeper water, and for the timing of sending Bob Goff at this critical juncture in our personal lives and our church's life to echo George's message with such joy and enthusiasm. Finally, Bob closed our prayer—*Amen*. Bob briefly kept his eyes locked on George and then joked: "We're going to need a mop—George is leaking Jesus all over the place!"

As a pastor, George was known as the consummate planner, sometimes sketching out sermons more than a year in advance. So it came as little surprise when we learned that shortly after doctors found the clear-cell tumor on his spine, George had decided to map out every detail—the scripture readings, the prayers, the music, *everything*—for his own memorial service, which he insisted be called "a Worship Service of Jesus Christ," not a funeral. Using his iPad, George recorded his own voice reading his selected scriptures and prayers. Then he created a "play list" with those voice recordings and his favorite worship songs in the precise order they would play at his memorial service. On George's most difficult nights, when sleep escaped him and pain and anxiety overwhelmed him, Pam sometimes awoke to find George with his eyes tightly closed and his headphones on, listening to his "Worship Service of Jesus Christ" on repeat.

On November 24, 2012, Jesus carried George home. Pam chose 2 Timothy 4:6-8 for the memorial service's program, which she felt perfectly captured her husband's life and ministry: "For I am already being poured out like a drink offering, and the time has come for my departure. I have fought the good fight, I have finished the race, I have kept the faith. Now there is in store for me the crown of righteousness, which the Lord, the righteous Judge, will award me on that day—and not only to me, but also to all who have longed for his appearing." It was truly a service of Christ-focused celebration—consistent with George's stubborn wishes, no one even spoke his name. As I listened to George's carefully selected readings, songs, and prayers, my deep reservoir of emotion brought up mostly happy tears. I imagined George joining his Lord and the chorus of angels, excitedly watching from heaven's balconies to see what we all would do next. I had no doubt that George was intently listening to his "Worship Service of Jesus Christ" and belting out his favorite hymns alongside us, his congregation. But now, he had no more pain or sleepless nights—just the best seat in the house.

CHAPTER 13

"He will wipe every tear from their eyes. There will be no more death or mourning or crying or pain, for the old order of things has passed away."
—REVELATION 21:4

We sometimes think of heaven as a faraway place, spatially and physically detached from us by an incalculable distance. This image may help us make some sense of an unknowable concept, but it finds little scriptural support. Throughout the Bible, God reinforces the notion that *he is with us*—here, now, and always: "When you pass through the waters, I will be with you" (Isaiah 43:2); "I am with you always, to the end of the age" (Matthew 28:20); "Behold, I am with you and will keep you wherever you go . . . I will not leave you until I have done what I promised you" (Genesis 28:15). In Acts 17:27-28, Paul stresses that God "is not far from any one of us"—indeed, it is *in God* that "we live and move and *have our being.*" As the writer Thomas Merton put it:

> Life is this simple. We are living in a world that is absolutely transparent, and God is shining through it all the time. This is not just a fable or a nice story. It is true. If we abandon ourselves to God and forget ourselves, we see it sometimes, and we see it maybe frequently. God shows himself everywhere, in everything—in people and in things and in nature and in events. It becomes very obvious that God is everywhere and in everything and we cannot be without him. It's impossible. The only thing is that we don't see it.

But sometimes, we *do* see it. In *The Heart of Christianity*, Marcus Borg discusses "thin places"—soul-stirring occurrences where heaven and earth seem to fleetingly converge and "the boundary between the two levels becomes very soft, porous, permeable"; where we're unmasked and, in a glimpse, God's goodness is unveiled; where we momentarily discard the worldly limitations and ambitions that too often define us and simply "behold God [and] experience the one in whom we live, all around us and within us." Thin places can be geographical locations (nature, your church, a relaxation spot), but they can also be much more—a person, a conversation, a seemingly chance encounter, a song; according to Borg, "anywhere our hearts are opened." They can be life-changing or serenely ordinary. But in every case, thin places jolt and disorient us, allowing us to reexamine our realities and reset our bearings.

Thin places can make the plain seem extraordinary. On an early Sunday morning in mid-November, 2010, I flew from Omaha into Chicago's Midway Airport and got on the train to head north for church in Ravenswood. I was near my all-time low: Beth's decision was still raw and unbearable, Amber's crash was fresh and her path to recovery unclear, and I was approaching the holiday season alone, with my life in complete disarray. I leaned on a pole near the railcar's door, ready for my stop, with a duffel bag in one hand and my Bible in the other. Sitting nearby was a man who I assumed was homeless. His layered, tattered shirts and coats gave off a pungent, bitter stench, and sprawling all around him were bags filled with aluminum cans and his personal belongings. Most sadly, the man had apparently lost his grip on reality. During our train ride, he alternated between snoozing and carrying on sad, heated conversations with a person who was not there.

Then, suddenly, the man looked directly at me. The tense, dramatic facial expressions that haunted his imaginary conversation melted away, and his eyes drifted to my Bible. "That's my favorite book!" the man said, grinning, with complete lucidity. A positive energy bubbled inside of me and made me shiver. "Oh yeah?" I said, politely smiling back. "Yeah," the man replied. "And let me tell you something—*God is real. He's _realer than real_*. Don't ever forget that." With those words, our train coasted to a stop, and the automated voice announced "This is Belmont"—my transfer station. I stumbled off in a clumsy daze, wishing the man well and wondering *what the heck just happened?* What followed was a curious, tingling euphoria that helped me through another hard day. Somehow, I felt God had met me in the train.

As I've probably already made clear, I can be painfully cynical, logical, and critical. If I were reading this book instead of writing it, by now I'd have tucked away in the corner of my mind a laundry list of rationalizations and interrogatories designed to dismantle or explain away the spiritual, often unverifiable, matters I've covered. Be that as it may, I *know* God has met me in these "thin places" where, from the depths of my fear, despair, and uncertainty, he showed me glimpses of hope, renewal, and salvation. In fact, it's by the boundless grace of God that he's gifted me these encounters, because without them, I'm not sure I'd be a Christian today—my skeptical nature is just too entrenched, and my faith too feeble.

God's mercy and compassion became *realer than real* to me at the intersection of 222nd and West Center Road when he heard me begging for a sign that my sister's spirit lived on and then called me four times from Kayla's hidden, buried cell phone. God's calming presence became *realer than real* to Amber on November 5, 2010, in the thin place where her life and death blurred and Kayla's spirit guarded her during the helicopter ride. God's healing power became *realer than real* when Amber gave a "thumbs-up" signifying the rebeginning of her consciousness after days of nothingness, and again a year later when Amber proudly exclaimed "*Ta-Da!*" while standing unassisted for the first time since her accident. God's guiding whispers became *realer than real* to shy Jenny when he nudged her to message me, a complete stranger, on Thanksgiving day—and when she listened to those whispers and started the conversation that would become our marriage. God's redemptive love became *realer than real* to me when Jenny—my "grace heaped on grace"—met me at the altar and a rabbit dashed by our feet, sitting perfectly between us. And God's eternal peace became *realer than real* to George in his final days, infusing him with strength and serenity that allowed him—with a tumor on his spine, stitches across his stomach, and no feeling in his legs—to praise God for his journey days before Jesus carried him home.

Of course, this isn't just a book about miracles. It's also a book about profound struggles and disappointments—death, drug dependency, self-image disorders, abuse, divorce, disability, and unanswered prayers. In my family's lives—as we see throughout scripture, and perhaps as you've seen in your own life—the joys and defeats often go hand-in-hand.

I believe God wants us to be happy. But I'm even more convinced that God desires for us to know him. To strip us of the masks and the comforts that distort our identities and dilute his higher call. To bring us to the thin places where he meets us, teaches us, and transforms us to be more like him. Where our utter reliance on God allows him to recalibrate our lives to finally pursue the purposes for which he made us. Where God whispers to us, if we abandon ourselves to him and listen closely, *"I love you; I am with you; you are mine."* And where we can finally see, through fleeting glimpses, his perfect nature: A God of awesome love. A God who delights in us with endless joy. A God of heaping grace. A God who is *realer than real*.

ACKNOWLEDGMENTS

I owe so many people so much.

I thank George, Pam, and my incredible friends, some of whom doubled as my editors, for carrying me through my trials and helping to rebuild me so I could write about this journey.

I thank my parents and Amber for letting me interview them and share their deeply personal histories in this book. Their choice to make themselves vulnerable by publicly exposing their most painful trials and deepest regrets is among the most difficult, courageous, and self-sacrificial decisions I've ever seen. They did it only to glorify God, trusting he will use their stories to change lives—or even save them.

I thank Jenny, who has been my constant cheerleader and sounding board throughout this book-writing journey—even as I touched on subjects from my past that were difficult for both of us to reflect on. Finding Jenny has helped me to believe in God's plan for me. Before, I thought random events and my life choices—where I was born, where I went to college or started working, etc.—dictated who I would meet and marry. But in Jenny, I found my *soulmate*, my perfect match—God's hand-chosen partner for me, uniquely knit through her nature and life experience, and woven into my life's fabric in such a way that allows us to best love, grow, balance, and complement each other. This had to happen in God's time, though—not ours. Just as Romans 5:3-5 asks us to rejoice in our hardships "because we know that suffering produces perseverance; perseverance, character; and character, hope," I now understand that before I could fulfill my half of the equation and become the man God intended for Jenny, I needed to endure and mature through my most severe disappointments—the very ones I begged God to take away from me. It was only by holding God's hand and walking through these storms that I could find Jenny's love waiting for me on the other side.

I thank Tom Osborne for reading my book and writing its foreword. His personal interest in this project has been one of my life's great honors.

I thank you, the reader, for buying this book. Half of its sales proceeds will fund a trust for the benefit of Amber and Bailey. On behalf of everyone in my family, _thank you_!

Finally, I thank God. For loving me, for listening to my prayers, for covering me in grace, and for having a plan for me. He is the source of everything good in my life. I am so blessed to be his child.

QUESTIONS TO CONSIDER

Chapter 1:
1. Consider the ways that your upbringing shaped you to be the person you are today. Which of your positive characteristics do you attribute to your upbringing? Are any less desirable components of your character traceable to your upbringing?
2. Who are the people in your past or present most responsible for your spiritual makeup today?
3. Looking back at the happiest times in your life and some of the lowest points, do you find any correlation—positive or negative—with your spiritual life?

Chapter 2:
1. What do you think happens when someone dies? What do you base this belief on? Does your belief depend on who the person is? Or what he or she has done in life? Or what he or she believes? Or something else?
2. Are there people in your life who, if you lost them today, you would feel regret over things you have said or done to them—or things you have not said or have not done?   What, if anything, are you willing to do about it now?

Chapter 3:
1. In your most difficult times, who tended to you, and how? Who in your life could you count on to help you through hard times today?
2. Do you know anyone who could use a pick-me-up right now?
3. Can you think of examples of times when you believe God answered your prayers? How about instances when you asked God for something, and it didn't turn out the way you prayed? Is it hard for you to reconcile these experiences?
4. What aspects of prayer are hardest for you to make sense of?

Chapter 4:
1. Are there negative parts of your past that weigh on you today? Is there someone in your life you can trust with this information, and who might be able to help you accept your past, learn from it, and move on constructively?
2. Do you know anyone who could benefit from the lessons you've learned the hard way?
3. Are you currently rationalizing or blinding yourself to any behaviors that you know are not right?
4. What does grace mean to you? In what ways has God shown you grace? How might you better show grace to others?

Chapter 5:
1. Throughout your life, what are some of the ways—positively or negatively—that you have tried to find meaning and self-value?
2. Are there any negative patterns in your life that you need to break free from?
3. What are the non-spiritual aspects of your life—your possessions, your job, etc.—that would be hardest for you to live without? Does this tell you anything about your priorities?
4. What steps can you take to make God a more intentional part of your day-to-day life?

Chapter 6:
1. Are there experiences in your life that have led you to feel angry with or skeptical of God? Have you shared these feelings with God or anyone else?
2. Do you have any unresolved feelings about past pains that may be affecting other areas of your life? What steps might you take to uncover and work through those feelings?
3. Consider relationships in your life that are broken or under stress. Do you see any patterns? What might you do differently for better future outcomes?
4. Are there any relationships in your life that could benefit from the unconditional love the Bible describes in 1 Corinthians 13—a love that is patient, kind, trusting, hopeful, and persevering, slow to anger, and keeps no record of wrongs? What are some practical ways you might better act out unconditional love in these relationships?

Chapter 7:
1. Have you ever been blessed by a stranger's random act of kindness? Are your eyes open for opportunities to encourage, help, or uplift the people you might encounter today?
2. In reflecting on the hardest moments of your life, did you feel then— or do you feel now—that God was with you? How was God working in those moments?

Chapter 8:
1. Have you seen God at work in another person's physical, emotional, or spiritual recovery?
2. Are there areas of your life where your inability to accept what *is*— rather than what you wish were the case—may be interfering with your growth and progress?
3. Are there areas of your life where you should consider loosening your control? What are some practical ways that you can hand these issues over to God?

Chapter 9:
1. Have you ever felt God "whispering" or "nudging" you to do or say something? Is there anything he might be trying to tell you today?
2. Have you ever exposed your personal "wounds" for the purpose of trying to help heal someone else? How was your gesture received? Was the experience a blessing to you, or difficult for you, or both?
3. What are the storms or crossroads in your life that you need God's strength to face and run through? Do you trust him to lead you?

Chapter 10:
1. Consider some of the major transitions you've experienced in your life. Did anyone or anything help stabilize your foundation during these life changes?
2. Identify an area of your life where you have matured or progressed over the years. What factors played a role in helping you make this positive change?
3. When and how have you experienced "grace heaped on grace"?
4. Think of the people who have figured most prominently and positively into your life. Do they know how much they mean to you?

Chapter 11:
1. Have you experienced redemption in your life in a personal and tangible way? How?

Chapter 12:
1. In what ways might God be calling you into deeper water in your walk with him?
2. Have you ever experienced God's grace in the midst of hardships? If so, how?
3. What emotions do you feel when you consider your own mortality? Are these emotions consistent or at odds with your spiritual beliefs?

Chapter 13:
1. What are the places or activities that bring you closest to God?
2. Have you seen God work in extraordinary ways?
3. Is there some ordinary way that God might use you to act out his love in someone else's life today?

CPSIA information can be obtained at www.ICGtesting.com
Printed in the USA
LVOW13s0015060813

346333LV00003B/3/P